How to *Really* Fool Yourself

How to Really Fool Yourself

Illusions for All Your Senses

Vicki Cobb

Illustrations by Jessica Wolk-Stanley

John Wiley & Sons, Inc.

New York   Chichester   Weinheim   Brisbane   Singapore   Toronto

Published by John Wiley & Sons, Inc.
Published simultaneously in Canada.
Illustrations by Jessica Wolk-Stanley
Figure on page 97 by Marvin L. Minsky and Seymour A. Papert.
Design and production by Navta Associates, Inc.

The publisher and the author have made every reasonable effort to ensure that the experiments and activities in this book are safe when conducted as instructed but assume no
responsibility for any damage caused or sustained while performing the experiments or
activities in the book. Parents, guardians, and/or teachers should supervise young read-
ers who undertake the experiments and activities in this book.

Library of Congress Cataloging-in-Publication Data:
Cobb, Vicki.
    How to really fool yourself : illusions for all your senses /
Vicki Cobb.
        p.   cm.
    Summary: Demonstrations accompanied by explanations illustrate how
and why the senses can be fooled.
        ISBN 0–471-31592–3 (paper : alk. paper)
        1. Senses and sensation—Juvenile literature.   2. Perception—Juvenile
literature.   3. Optical illusions—Juvenile literature.   [1. Senses and
sensation.   2. Perception.   3. Optical illusions.]   I. Title.
QP434.C56   1998
612.8—dc21   98-27723

Printed in the United States of America

10   9   8   7   6   5   4   3   2   1

Contents

A Sense of Reality

AT THIS VERY MOMENT you are having an experience with this book. You are reading these words, and, if you are holding the book in your hands, you are feeling its weight and the smoothness of its pages. You may be aware of its smell. All true. So what else is new?

Seriously, how do you know that this book exists? That it is not a figment of your imagination? That it is not an illusion? In your perception, this book is real! Here's a list of reality checks to prove it:

1 You can see it.

2 You can touch it and feel its weight.

3 You can smell it and maybe taste it.

4 You can read it aloud and hear the words.

5 You can ask other people if they experience these same reality checks, thus confirming your own.

In short, you test for reality by bombarding all your senses with various aspects of the experience of this moment. If they agree, you have a sense of reality.

A Subject to Question

What is reality, really? Three separate views of reality are nicely illustrated in a joke. Three baseball umpires are stating how they each judge balls and strikes. The first umpire says, "I calls 'em as I sees 'em." (He trusts his sense of sight to show him what is real.) The second umpire, feeling much superior to the first, says, "I calls 'em as they is!" (His judgments based on his sense of sight are real.) The third umpire, certain he is one up on the other two, smiles and says in resounding tones, "They ain't nothin' 'til I calls 'em!" (His personal judgments create reality. Where the ball actually is located in the strike zone doesn't count.)

The question of reality has fascinated philosophers, psychologists, scientists, writers, and other seekers of truth for all of recorded history. In discussions and writings, they have considered such heavy questions as: What is existence? ("To be or not to be?") What is awareness? ("I think, therefore I am.") If a tree fell in the forest and nobody heard it, did it make a sound? These questions are fair game for anyone to argue. Try one. There is no final authority on the answers, and the solutions are still up for grabs. But as far as your reality experience of this book is concerned and the experience of its content still to come, I suggest that reality has three parts.

The first part is made up of the book's physical properties and the physical properties of the rest of the universe that are separate from you. The book's physical properties include its size, shape, weight, light reflecting from its surfaces, sounds of words read aloud, and the chemical makeups of paper and ink. Physical properties to which a person responds are called *stimuli.* (A single property responded to is a *stimulus.*)

The second part of reality is *sensation*—the various ways your body reacts to external stimuli or events. These responses occur first in specialized sense organs—eyes, ears, nose, and skin—that all have one thing in common, namely, nerve cells. Nerve cells that respond to stimuli are called *receptors,* and they carry messages of stimuli to the brain.

Receptors in your eyes are, of course, sensitive to light. Vision is considered our dominant sense if you go by the numbers. Seventy percent of all receptor cells in your body are in your eyes. Sound is sensed primarily by your ears, although your skin has been known to sense certain sound vibrations. Your nose and mouth have receptors sensitive to *chemicals.* Receptors fire messages to the brain when they make direct contact with certain molecules. Our chemical sense of smell and taste are considered our most primitive senses. Other animals, including dogs and fish, are far more developed in this area than we are. Basic survival in many lower animals depends more on these senses than in our case. And, finally, there is your skin and internal touch receptors, which respond to temperature, pressure, and pain in such an infinite variety of combinations that you know when a fly is walking along your arm, when you are touching velvet, and when a pot is too hot to handle. The marvel of touch led the great Greek philosopher Aristotle to think of it as the most important sense. For him, touch was the ultimate test of reality. If you could touch something, it was truly real.

The third part of reality is knowledge gained from your past experiences. How your sense organs responded to stimuli in the past, how your brain interpreted the information, how you behaved, and the consequences of your actions all play a part in your present experience. The thousands of hours you spent learning to speak English, then learning to read it, then learning that some books are a pleasant experience, are no small part of the reality of this moment (I hope!).

About Fooling Yourself

Perception is the awareness that comes from the stimuli of the physical world, your sensation of them, and your experience in interpreting them. Perception is your basic way of knowing reality. But, although your perceptions *seem* accurate, they are often subject to weaknesses and limits. You are susceptible to illusions, to *not* experiencing reality accurately, yet experiencing something that appears and feels very real. When you are aware of a misperception, you feel strange. Your mind tells you that your senses are deceiving you. The word "illusion" comes from a Latin root meaning "mockery." Your eyes and ears can play tricks on you. So can your other senses.

This is what this book is about: ways to explore the weaknesses and limits of your perception, ways to create all kinds of illusions for yourself, setting up contradictory situations where your senses tell you one message and your brain tells you another. There are many reasons why illusions occur. Some are caused by built-in limits of your senses. Some are based on conflicts between senses. Some come from false expectations. And some are in the physical world itself.

If there is any lesson to be learned in life, it is that we can make mistakes. Judgments based on false perceptions can be errors. (Unfortunately, they can also prove correct.) The experiments in fooling yourself in this book show one important thing: most of us perceive in similar ways, and our perceptions are similarly leading us astray.

These illusions and experiments can be experienced by all of us. Sometimes it takes a little time and practice to have the experience. So, if you don't "get" an illusion right away, keep trying.

Throughout the history of science, it has been extremely useful to know how we can be fooled. By knowing our weaknesses and limitations, we created tools to correct and extend them. Instruments like the telescope and microscope clearly extend the limits of our senses. Computers have memories that make no mistakes when it comes to total recall. Great minds create models of never-seen objects like atoms and molecules that can explain events we do experience. Such ideas create another reality that helps us to understand the universe and leads to a different kind of truth. Awareness of how we can be mistaken helps us stop kidding ourselves.

Maybe our biggest illusion is that we must be right all the time. If so, you've come to the right place. This book is an adventure in human failing. Prepare yourself for many humbling yet enlightening experiences. Enjoy!

Weird Feelings

ARISTOTLE (384-322 B.C.), the Greek philosopher, was the first to state that the human body had only five senses. He called our fifth sense "touch," although he wasn't sure that this was a single sense like sight, hearing, smell, and taste. Modern thought on touch has come up with so many subdivisions and qualities that understanding this sense is difficult, if not confusing. Some of these qualities include pressure, contact, deep pressure, muscle strain, prickly pain, deep pain, quick pain, warmth, cold, dizziness, hunger, thirst, itch, tickle, and vibration.

More than two thousand years after Aristotle, touch is still our most mysterious sense. Unlike our other senses, which have specific locations within our bodies, touch is located in two square yards of skin and in deeper underlying muscles and organs. Scientists have isolated and studied four different kinds of nerves in our skin that seem to be individually sensitive to warmth, cold, pressure, and pain, although there is some confusion as to which nerves are responsible for which feelings. The most popular current theory about touch is that the different qualities are the result of different patterns of nerve firings. A nerve firing is measured in laboratories as an electrical impulse along a nerve fiber. Different kinds of stimuli cause different receptors to fire. Different combinations of nerve firings produce different sensations. Despite the tremendous amount of research on touch done in the last one hundred years, most researchers agree that we are only beginning to perceive the depth of our ignorance.

Where there is some understanding, I'll tell you about it. Where an explanation is still waiting to be discovered, I'll just present the illusion. Perhaps you can dream up your own experiments to explore these mysteries. Often what seems to be an explanation is perhaps just another description of what's happening. One thing, however, is certain: the experiments and illusions in this chapter will make you feel that what's happening is pretty weird.

Aristotle's Illusion

Feel two noses on your face.

Since Aristotle felt that touch was the most important sense for detecting reality, this touch illusion is named for him.

How to Fool Yourself

Cross the middle finger over the index finger of your favorite hand as if you're going to tell a lie. (Your hand, as you will see, is going to lie to you.) Run the tips of your crossed fingers up and down your nose so that the sides of the **V** made by the tips are each touching one side of your nose. Feel the space between your "noses" get wider, especially toward the tip. Closing your eyes helps to create the illusion.

Why You're Fooled

Aristotle's illusion belongs to a class of illusions called "misplaced assumptions." You have spent a lifetime getting information from your fingertips when they are in an uncrossed position. You know where they are when you feel things. When you cross your fingertips, you change their ordinary relationship to each other, and your brain is confused. You interpret the sensation as if your fingers were in their usual position.

There are variations on this. Feel a marble with crossed fingers or run them up and down a pencil. You will feel two of everything you touch. Rest your index finger on top of a friend's index finger. Feel both fingers with your other hand by running your index finger and thumb along their length. You expect to feel something different from what you are actually feeling. Some kids I know call this feeling "Dead Man's Skin."

Give Yourself a Lift

Feel your arms rise all by themselves without your making them move.

How to Fool Yourself

In this illusion you feel as if your body has a will of its own. Motion that normally takes some effort becomes effortless.

First, give yourself a basis for comparison. Stand up and raise both arms outward from your sides. Feel their weight and the strain in your muscles.

Now stand in a doorway, your hands hanging down, your palms facing your body. Move your hands outward and press the backs of your hands against the doorframe. Strain your muscles as you press hard and count slowly to thirty. Your arms will shake a little with the effort.

At the end of the count step forward away from the doorway and let your arms relax completely by your sides. Your arms will rise as if you were going to take off in flight without any work on your part.

Why You're Fooled

When you are pressing the backs of your hands against the doorframe, your muscles contract as if you are raising your arms. The doorframe prevents your arms from actually rising. When you step forward, you remove the obstacle, but your muscles continue to contract, thus raising your arms. This effect is like the persistent afterimage of vision (see chapter 7). If you lift a heavy weight and then lift a light one, your judgment about how heavy the second weight is will have been altered by the previous experience. The second weight will seem much lighter. For this reason baseball players swing several bats while warming up. When they step up to the plate, the single bat will seem so much lighter by comparison that they will swing it more quickly, thus giving the ball more impact if they connect.

Lightweight Thinking

*A smaller object feels heavier than a larger one
when they are both the same weight.*

How to Fool Yourself

Which weighs more—a pound of feathers or a pound of gold? Many people are fooled by this riddle and answer "a pound of gold" because gold seems "heavier" (it's actually denser) than feathers.

You don't need gold and feathers to check this out for yourself. I picked out two items from the pantry—a small metal container of ground ginger and a box of instant onion soup. They weighed exactly the same on my postal scale. Any two items of significantly different sizes that weigh the same will do. I gave both items to friends and family and asked which was heavier. Everyone lifted both and, without exception, said that the metal box was heavier.

Why You're Fooled

Experience teaches us that, in general, smaller objects weigh less than larger ones. We expect the smaller object to be lighter than the larger one. When we lift both, our expectations are not met, and the result is that the smaller object feels heavier. This explanation, however, has its problems. The illusion persists even when we know that they are the same weight and when we lift both with our eyes closed.

Obviously, the explanation of this illusion is worthy of deep and weighty consideration.

The Incredible Shrinking Cube

*Feel a sugar cube grow smaller as you hold it
between your fingers.*

How to Fool Yourself

You'll need a magnifying glass, a handkerchief, and a sugar cube, die, or other small cube. Cover your favorite hand with the handkerchief. Actively feel the cube through the handkerchief with your thumb and index and middle fingers while looking at it through the magnifying glass. Keep it up for several minutes, making sure that your fingers are pressing the distinct edges and corners of the cube. Then close your eyes and keep feeling the cube. After several seconds, the cube seems to shrink. This illusion may take a few tries before you experience it, but the incredible effect is well worth the effort.

Why You're Fooled

Vision is our dominant sense. When we get conflicting information at the same time from touch and vision, we perceive what we see, not what we feel. A cube viewed through a magnifying glass looks larger than it really is, and you feel it as the size you *see* it. When you remove vision and only receive information through touch, you perceive the size of the cube as it really is.

The size of your fingers is another clue to the size of things held in the hand. The handkerchief prevents you from seeing your fingers, which can destroy the illusion.

What's the Point?

*Your skin feels as if it's being poked with one point
when it's actually being poked with two.*

How to Fool Yourself

Get a large hairpin or open a paper clip to form a **V**. Have the points about an inch apart. Close your eyes and press both points against the back of your hand. Do you feel one point or two? Now press both points against your back. It will feel as if only one point is sticking you.

What is the smallest distance between the two points that allows you to feel both points? Is this distance the same for different parts of the body? Check it out with a friend—one of you be the subject and the other be the experimenter. The experimenter touches sometimes one point and sometimes two to different parts of the subject's body. The subject is blindfolded and must state whether he or she feels one or two points. Vary the distance between points. You'll find that different parts of the body are more, or less, sensitive in accurately determining if the stimulus is made up of one or two points.

Why You're Fooled

A great deal of research has gone into studying the sensitivity of the body in determining the distance between two points. One study showed that the middle finger is the most sensitive of the five fingers. It felt two points when they were only 2.5 millimeters (¼ inch) apart. The calf was the least sensitive. Two distinct separate points were first felt when they were 47 millimeters (about 2½ inches) apart.

Scientists also mapped the parts of the brain that corresponded to various parts of the body. The size of the brain area that responded to the forearm was the same as that of the thumb. In other words, the thumb, which is much more sensitive than the forearm, took up as much space in the brain as the entire forearm did.

Cold Reality . . . or Hot?

*One hand feels warm water and the
other cool water in the same pot.*

How to Fool Yourself

Get three large bowls or pots. Fill one with water that is about room temperature. Put ice water in another pot and hot water (as hot as you can comfortably stand) in the third. Hold one hand in the hot water and the other in the ice water for thirty seconds. Then plunge both hands into the water that is at room temperature. The tepid water will feel warm to the hand that's been in ice water and cool to the hand that was in hot water. So, your sensation depends on where each hand is coming from.

Why You're Fooled

This illusion was the basis for an extended discussion on the subject of reality by the famous French mathematician and philosopher René Descartes (1596–1650). He concluded from this experiment and other observations that trusting your senses was *not* the way to know reality. True reality came only from ideas, including the idea of doubting one's senses. That's why he said, "I think, therefore I am." His awareness of himself defined existence and reality.

Here's What's Wet

Your hands are dry, yet they feel wet.

How to Fool Yourself

Put on a rubber glove and plunge your hand into cold water. If you didn't know you had gloves on, you'd swear your hand was wet. Now try warm water. The feeling is not so pronounced. The sensation of "wetness," according to scientists, has two components. One is coldness, and the other is pressure evenly distributed over an area of skin.

Why You're Fooled

The skin is one of the most sensitive and reliable information-gathering organs we have. Correct judgments are often made on the basis of feel alone. We correctly identify properties such as hardness, softness, smoothness, roughness, stickiness, greasiness, wetness, and dryness. Scientists have tried to figure out the parts of each special feeling with very little success up to now. They suggest that many of these sensations are the result of "touch blends." Theoretically, if you have broken down the components of a touch blend such as wetness, for example, you should be able to simulate the feeling by putting them back together without using something that's wet. Cold water perceived through a rubber glove also gives an even pressure and makes you feel as if your hand was wet even though it's dry.

Here are some analyses of other skin "feelings." See if you can think up ways to create these feelings artificially.

- Hardness—even, cold pressure with a distinct boundary
- Softness—uneven, warm pressure with no distinct boundary
- Stickiness—uneven, moving, jerky pressure

This is one area that's wide open for groundbreaking discoveries. So go for it!

A Sense of Horror

Feel dead eyeballs, brains, and a heart—only kidding!

How to Fool Yourself

Close your eyes, add a little imagination, and feel dead parts of the human body. These illusions are the stuff of Halloween and haunted houses. Think grim and macabre thoughts while caressing the following foods: cold, wet grapes are great eyeballs; cold, wet, cooked macaroni feels like brains might feel. Plunge a whole tomato into boiling water for about twenty seconds. Then peel off the skin. Chill in the refrigerator. Hold the cold, peeled tomato and imagine that it's a heart.

Share these weird and horrible sensations with your friends. (Isn't that what friends are for?) Try them on your parents and siblings.

Why You're Fooled

The best way to set up the illusion is to tell a blindfolded person that he or she will be feeling dead organs. Then plunge the victim's hand into the bowl. What you've done is set up a learned expectation. But do it quickly, so your victim doesn't have time to think about it.

The common quality of all these materials is *clamminess.* Scientists have described clamminess as "a cold softness felt with movement and accompanied by unpleasant mental pictures." Some scientists believe that the emotions of anxiety, love, and disgust are simple skin sensations (that we know are not at all simple) along with changes in internal chemistry. Perhaps deep feeling is not so deep after all. Love, along with horror, may be only skin deep.

How to Keep from Kidding Yourself

*A swinging pendulum can reveal
your innermost feelings.*

How to Fool Yourself

How well do you know yourself? You may have secret desires that you are not aware of. Maybe you *are* fooling yourself and don't know it. Here's a stunt that tells you what you *really* think. Maybe. You'll need to make a pendulum by tying a weight on the end of a ten-inch string.

Let the weight hang freely. Hold the end of the string as steady as possible. A circular motion by the pendulum bob means "yes" and a back-and-forth motion means "no." Start asking yourself questions and observe the motion of the bob. Some questions might be: "Do I really like _____?" "Do I want _____ to happen?" Then try some questions where the answer is obvious just to see how accurate the pendulum swings are: "Is my name_____?" See if you get a correct response.

Why You're Fooled

Everyone has muscle tension that is too small to detect easily. Such tension is called "covert" because it is covered or hidden. The motion of the pendulum magnifies tiny muscular movements, thus revealing covert muscular responses to the questions you ask yourself.

Try this one out on friends. Make sure that they try to hold the pendulum as steady as possible. Give each answer time to develop.

No Sign of a Signature

Completely destroy your ability to sign your name.

Sit at a table with a pencil and paper. Depending on whether you are right- or left-handed, use your favored foot to trace circles on the floor. Once you get your foot going, watch it to make certain it keeps moving in a circle. Now try to sign your name. The scrawl you produce will make you feel helpless. If you do succeed in signing your name fairly legibly, chances are that your foot has traced similar motions. You have not kept it moving in a circle.

Why You're Fooled

The muscle coordination problem here is similar to rubbing your stomach and patting your head at the same time. One set of motions competes with the other and interferes with either one's being done successfully. With practice, however, it is possible to master this one. Some weird people may think it's worth the effort.

Master Mirror Writing

You can write backwards.

How to Fool Yourself

Here's a way to fool yourself into doing something you think is impossible. Hold half a piece of paper against your forehead. Place the tip of a pencil (a ballpoint will not write for long at this angle) on the paper on the left side of your forehead. In cursive writing (with all the letters linked) write a word or a phrase such as "hello" or "I love you." Write quickly, imagining that the paper is in front of you. Don't stop to think about what you are doing.

When you are finished, look at the paper. You markings will be about as meaningful as hieroglyphics. However, if you turn the paper over and hold it up to the light, or if you hold it up to a mirror, the writing will be readable.

Why You're Fooled

When you write in this position, your right and left brain get confused, and you automatically reverse the writing motion that's in your muscle memory. A few people (Leonardo da Vinci was one) can do mirror writing. But most people can't.

A Whirling World

Feel the earth move beneath your feet when you're standing still.

How to Fool Yourself

Hold a baseball bat, handle up, on the floor. Put your forehead on the base of the handle. Walk around the bat three times. Now stand up straight and tell yourself the earth is not moving. That should do it.

Why You're Fooled

What you have done has destroyed your sense of balance. An expert on dizziness gave me this method and said that it was the zonker of all time.

Your sense of balance is controlled by three tubelike canals in each of your inner ears. When the fluid in the canals is set in motion, you experience dizziness. Spinning around with your head up will set this fluid in motion in one direction. But when you place your head in another position and then turn around, you create all kinds of unusual motion that makes everything seem to tilt and spin. Fortunately, the effect is temporary.

Strange Sounds
and a Taste for
the Mysterious

PEOPLE WHO BECOME LOST in the woods have been known to wander about in large circles thinking that they are walking in a straight line. They have the illusion that their sense of direction is accurate. The reality is that hearing is a far more reliable sense for finding your way out of such circumstances than a "sense of direction." Hearing is important for perceiving distance and direction. The best way to find civilization is to walk toward a sound, such as a brook or highway. You know when you are getting nearer because the sound gets louder.

Our ears are amazing devices for detecting an enormous variety of sounds. Inside our ears are thin, sensitive membranes—eardrums—that respond to sound. Sound is created by vibrating air that presses against our eardrums, setting them in motion. The motion of our eardrums is then translated into nerve impulses to the brain through a complex series of events. The range of the ear's sensitivity is enormous. We hear the simplest sounds, such as tones from a tuning fork, including high ones and low ones. We enjoy the complexities of the organized sound of music and the subtle difference in voices. Our brain focuses attention on different kinds of sound. We can pick up the soft sound of a pin dropping, when we pay attention, and yet tune out loud background noise that would interfere with concentration.

Much of the time we are fooled by the ways we interpret sounds. If you are alone at night, you may hear all kinds of spooky sounds. More often than not, it's your imagination (your brain, not your ears) working overtime.

Your chemical senses of taste and smell can also be fooled. The receptors for taste are located in bumps, called taste buds, on your tongue, along your throat, and on the roof of your mouth. They fire when molecules from food in your saliva come in contact with them. The receptors for smell are found in the lining of the upper part of the cavity inside the nose. They also fire when molecules come in contact with them.

Smell is remarkable for two reasons. First, it is extremely sensitive. Some scientists estimate that smell is 10,000 times more sensitive than taste. It responds to extremely small numbers of molecules. Second, smell is the fastest-adapting of all our senses. You've noticed this when you come across a strong and unpleasant odor. Within a few minutes you'll adapt and no longer notice the smell.

Smell and taste are very closely associated. Without smell you would have very little appreciation for fine cooking. Taste would be limited to the basic flavors, which are sweet, salty, bitter, and sour. Remove smell, and you can be fooled by taste alone. The taste of foods is also affected by the sense of touch. The texture and temperature of foods—the way food feels in your mouth—is also a part of your perception and can be part of an a illusion.

Illusions of hearing and the chemical senses are fascinating, but there are not too many of them compared to vision. For this reason, I've put them in one chapter. Hear and taste the unreal.

Hear a Sound and Know Not Where

You can't tell where a sound is coming from.

Sit blindfolded on a stool in the middle of a room without moving your head. Have three friends take turns clapping hands above your head, in front of you, and behind you. The clapper should be careful to make no other noise and be far enough away so that you can't detect any moving air from the clap. The claps should be on an imaginary line over the center of your head so that they are the same distance to each ear. You will not be able to tell where the clap is coming from.

Why You're Fooled

Sound localization depends on sound's reaching each ear at slightly different times. This occurs when the distance to a sound is slightly different for each ear, so the sound takes a fraction of a second longer to reach one ear than the other. When a sound is the same distance from both ears, reaching both ears at the same instant, you will not be able to locate it. Turning your head or cocking it creates unequal distances between your ears and the sound source, helping you find its direction.

Vision can also confuse your ability to locate sounds. There is a study that demonstrates this. The person who was the subject in the study was seated on a stool, feet off the ground, with his head held in a brace so that it couldn't be moved. He was surrounded by a shower curtain that had vertical stripes. The shower curtain rotated so that the stripes passed in front of his eyes. A sound made directly in front of the face, but behind the moving curtain, seemed to be coming from directly overhead.

The moving curtain created the illusion of motion (see chapter six). Vertical stripes passing in front of the eyes make you feel as if you are moving along in a direction opposite to the motion of the stripes. The moving stripes make you feel as if you are moving past the point you are facing.

Past experience teaches that sound changes with motion. Sounds, such as a siren or train whistle, always change in pitch as you pass them or they pass you. If you have a visual illusion of motion, you *know* a sound you appear to be passing *cannot* remain unchanged. So you resolve the conflict by perceiving the sound that's actually in front of you as if it were coming from directly above.

Sounds of the Sea

Hear the ocean roar far from the sea.

How to Fool Yourself

Listen to the opening in a seashell. (If you haven't one handy, put your ear against an empty jar.) The sound of the surf crashing against the shore is loud and clear.

Why You're Fooled

Noise from your environment, including noise made by your ear's brushing against the edge of the shell or jar, is reinforced by the vibration of the air inside the shell or jar. This enhanced sound, called *resonance,* seems very much like the distant roar of the ocean.

Sound Effects

Create all kinds of sounds with ordinary objects.

How to Fool Yourself

Radio, the theater, and movies simulate sounds for dramatic effect. A lot of sound effects now are created by computers, but many still use natural sounds as their bases. Here's a list of some of the ways early sound technicians created environmental sounds. Experiment with them. Some require electronic equipment. If you have a microphone and speaker, you can experiment with direct amplification. If you have a tape recorder, tape your sound effects and then play them back. If no electronic equipment is available, close your eyes and imagine that you're hearing the real thing.

Rain—Take your choice: put about ¼ cup dried peas in a metal pie pan. Gently move the peas around the pan with a circular motion. Pour sand or rice against a Ping-Pong ball. Make a chute of waxed paper and pour a trickle of sugar along it from the top so that it runs down the chute.

Wind—Pull a silk (or polyester) scarf across the back of a chair. For wind in the trees, shake some tinsel near a microphone.

Thunder—Breathe gently on a microphone. Shake a flexible cookie sheet from one corner. The best effect by far is made by holding up one end of a large plastic chair mat (used to protect carpets under an office chair) and shaking it.

Ocean waves—Put an assortment of dried peas or rice and some gravel in a vinyl suitcase. Close the case. Rhythmically lift each end so that the contents swish along the case and crash at the end.

Fire—Crumple a large piece of cellophane in front of a microphone.

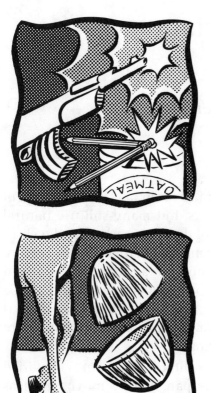

Foghorn—Blow across the mouth of an empty soda bottle. You can raise the pitch by adding a little water. (Combine this one with the waves and you've created the seashore.)

Gunshot—Whack a ruler against the back of a leather chair or against a wood surface.

Machine gun—Drum rapidly with an irregular beat with two pencils on the bottom of an empty oatmeal box.

Explosion—Burst a paper bag while recording at the fastest speed your recorder is capable of and play it back at the slowest speed.

Waterfall—Record water running from your faucet at a high speed and play it back at a slow one.

Train—Rhythmically rub two sandpaper blocks together, slowly picking up speed.

Hoofbeat—This is a classic effect. It takes a bit of practice to get the rhythm right, but the source is two halves of a coconut shell (small wooden salad bowls also work). The beat is a rapid triplet with the emphasis on the final beat—t-da-dub, t-da-dub. The horse sounds as if it's running on pavement if you drum the shells against the bathroom floor. If you drum against a padded surface, the horse sounds as if it's running on grass.

Jet plane—Use a hair dryer and make the engines howl by covering the exhaust with your hand.

Footsteps in the snow—Fill a small plastic bag with flour. Rhythmically strike it against a hard surface.

A voice on the telephone—Speak into a small plastic cup.

Why You're Fooled

Sound illusions depend almost entirely on the listener's past experiences. All of the illusions above have some of the same components of the real sounds, enough to create the illusions.

How to Keep a Secret

You can't hear a whisper from a friend sitting next to you.

How to Fool Yourself

Sit back-to-back with a friend. One of you whispers a secret message. The other can't hear it. This works much better outside than inside. Outside, a whisper made facing away from you is impossible to understand even if it is spoken as loudly as a normal speaking voice.

Why You're Fooled

Sound travels in waves that bend around objects much as water waves bend around small objects on their surface. Sound waves of the low tones of a normal speaking voice bend easily around the speaker's head. That's why you can hear what's said when the speaker faces away from you.

Sound waves from a whisper, however, are not as easily bent. They don't travel around the speaker so that they can be heard as words in a message. Sounds of whispers do bounce off walls, which is why you can't do this trick inside. In fact, the way whispers bounce off walls, which is different from speaking-voice echoes, creates another illusion in whispering galleries. A person can whisper in one part of the gallery, and someone on the other side hears it as if it is coming from a nearby place. In a whispering gallery a secret can be told from across the room, and the receiver is nowhere near the teller.

How Not to Keep a Secret

See how a message changes as it passes from person to person.

How to Fool Yourself

Gather as many friends as you can—at least ten. Stand or sit them in a line. Write a message on a piece of paper. Make it a simple statement. Whisper your message to the first person, who then passes it on to the next, and so on. After the words have been "processed" by each member of the group, have the last person repeat the message. Compare it to the one you wrote down. The odds are high that they will not be exactly the same. This phenomenon is the basis for the game "Rumor."

Why You're Fooled

People hear selectively. They pay attention to what is familiar to them, and they substitute new words (or omit one or two) according to their own understanding of a message.

The difference between the original message and the final result is not a single perceptual illusion. It is the sum of each person's misperception. If there's any lesson to be learned here, it is that you and your friends are not a recording machine. This is the reason that hearsay evidence is not admissible in a court of law—it is likely to be inaccurate. You cannot repeat what someone else told you and have it accepted as evidence.

What's That Again?

Here's a list of misstatements that sound hilarious when read out loud.

How to Fool Yourself

Did you ever learn to recite something as a very young child, only to learn years later that you were saying the wrong thing? Only when we read what we've been saying can we realize our misconceptions.

"*I led the pigeons* to the flag…"	(I pledge allegiance to the flag…)
"…and to the republic for *Richie Stans*…"	(…and to the republic for which it stands…)
"…one *naked individual*…"	(…one nation indivisible…)
"Our Father, who art in heaven, *Harold* be thy name…"	(hallowed be thy name…)
"…and lead us not into *Penn Station*…"	(temptation)
"*Shirley, good Mrs. Murphy* shall follow me all the days of my life…"	(Surely goodness and mercy…)
Neck store neighbor or *next store* neighbor	(next-door neighbor)
"The Star-Spangled Banana" or "The Stars-Bangled Banger"	("The Star-Spangled Banner")

Why You're Fooled

Double talk is words that sound like English but don't make any sense. The master of double talk was Lewis Carroll, who wrote the poem "Jabberwocky" in *Through the Looking-Glass*. Here's the first verse that sounds really meaningful with the proper inflections:

> *'Twas brillig, and the slithy toves*
> *Did gyre and gimble in the wabe:*
> *All mimsy were the borogoves,*
> *And the mome raths outgrabe.*

An Illusion Worth Repeating

*You can't prevent a repeated word
from becoming another word.*

How to Fool Yourself

You may think you can repeat a simple word aloud and it will stay the same word no matter how many times you say it. But it won't. Say the word "say" over and over again rapidly. At some point it will become the word "ace." It will stay "ace" for a while and then shift abruptly back to "say."

Why You're Fooled

Scientists call this phenomenon "verbal alternation." It is similar to the shifting perception of ambiguous visual forms like the Necker cube on page 46. There are many words that will alternate if you repeat them aloud rapidly. Try the word "rest." It will become "tress" and may become "Esther." You have no control over the alternating form the word takes. You are unconsciously reorganizing certain speech sounds to produce different words.

Wood You Could Taste

Discover how tasteless wood acquires a flavor.

How to Fool Yourself

Use the handle of a wooden spoon (the bowl of the spoon may have taken on the taste of sauces it has stirred), a wooden coffee stirrer or a clean ice-cream stick, or a doctor's tongue depressor. Press the wooden stimulator to different parts of the tongue—the tip, the sides, the back. See if the wood takes on one of the four basic tastes—sweet, sour, salty, or bitter—depending on where you touch it.

Why You're Fooled

As mentioned earlier, taste receptors are located in the bumps on your tongue called taste buds. Different taste buds are responsible for the different basic tastes. Although taste buds for all four tastes are located all over the tongue, there are more sweet receptors on the tip, more sour on the sides, and more bitter in the back. Salt receptors seem more evenly distributed than the others.

The person who told me about this illusion claims that the mechanical stimulation by a tasteless object fires the receptors, making it appear to have a taste. When I tried it with different people, I got different results. Some people were more sensitive than others.

Flavorless Coffee

Eliminate the distinctive flavor of coffee in your mouth.

How to Fool Yourself

Hold your nose and put a few grains of fresh coffee grounds in your mouth. Chew them. Now open your nose. Suddenly the characteristic flavor of coffee fills your mouth.

Why You're Fooled

This experiment shows how important your sense of smell is for experiencing full flavors. Receptors in your nose respond to all kinds of molecules your taste buds are incapable of responding to.

Now you know why preparing gourmet food for someone with a cold is wasted effort.

Name That Food

An apple, a raw potato, and an onion all taste alike.

How to Fool Yourself

Put on a blindfold and nose clips. (You can hold your nose, if you keep it airtight.) Have a friend place a small piece of one of the above three foods on your tongue. Guess what it is just from the taste without chewing. (The texture is another clue that can give it away.)

Why You're Fooled

You will make mistakes because, again, it's largely differences in their odors which make them taste different.

See if you can tell the difference between Coke and 7-Up. A blindfold and nose clips make it almost impossible. The beverages taste surprisingly alike. They are both lemon-lime based drinks, although one is sweeter than the other. You'll have no problem telling them apart with your senses of smell and vision operating.

False Sweetness

Make water taste sweet without putting any sweetener into it.

How to Fool Yourself

Shake some salt on one side of your tongue. Give it a minute to become sensitive to the taste. Now put water on the other side of your tongue. (Use a spoon to dribble it over the surface.) How does the water taste? I found that it was definitely sweet. If the water is slightly sweetened, it will now taste very sweet.

Wash a fresh artichoke by running water through it and turning it upside down to drain. Wrap it tightly in cellophane wrap. Microwave it on high 7 to 8 minutes. The center should feel tender when you stick a fork into it. Remove the leaves to expose the heart. Cut off the bristlelike choke.

Chew a quarter of the heart and hold it in your mouth for one minute. Now drink some water or milk. It will have a sweet flavor. You'll find the same effect from eating the leaves.

Why You're Fooled

Salt makes your taste buds especially sensitive to other tastes. A tasteless substance, like water, acquires a sweet taste when part of the tongue is stimulated with salt. People salt melons and grapefruit because a little salt makes them taste sweeter.

Artichokes contain a chemical that alters the receptors on your tongue so that water or milk will taste sweet. Chemists are trying to isolate the chemical in artichokes that produces this effect for use as an artificial sweetener. Fine chefs do not like to serve vintage wines with artichokes because the true flavor of the wine cannot be appreciated by an artichoke-doctored tongue.

Food That's Almost the Real Thing

Taste meatless chopped liver and hamburgers and an apple-less apple pie. Amazing!

How to Fool Yourself

Prepare the following recipes:

FAKE CHOPPED LIVER

½ cup chopped celery
1 chopped onion
¼ cup oil

5 hard-boiled eggs
4 ounces chopped walnuts
salt, pepper, garlic powder to taste

1 Brown the celery and onions in the oil.

2 Chop or grind browned celery and onions, eggs, and walnuts in a wooden chopping bowl, food processor, or meat grinder.

3 Season with salt, pepper, and garlic powder.

Serve chilled on crackers or on a bed of lettuce with a slice of tomato.

FAKE HAMBURGERS

½ pound lentils
1 tablespoon butter
1 small onion, chopped
½ cup rough vegetable protein
(can be purchased at any
health food store)

2 eggs
salt, pepper, garlic powder to taste
cracker meal
cooking oil or margarine

1 Simmer lentils in a partly covered saucepan, with enough water to cover, over a low flame for one hour. Drain well and place in a large mixing bowl.

2   Brown the chopped onion in butter. Add to the lentils.

3   Add rough vegetable protein, raw eggs, and seasoning. Mix well, with clean hands.

4   Form into patties and coat with cracker meal by placing each patty on some meal in a dish.

5   Heat the oil or margarine in a skillet until hot. Cook the patties about 5 minutes on each side.

Serve hot with ketchup. A hamburger roll and a slice of raw onion add to the illusion.

MOCK APPLE PIE

This is a humdinger of an illusion. No one will believe that this pie is not made of apples but Nabisco's RITZ crackers.

pastry for a two-crust pie (frozen is fine)
36 RITZ crackers
2 cups water
2 cups sugar

2 teaspoons cream of tartar
2 tablespoons lemon juice
grated rind of one lemon
butter or margarine

1 Preheat the oven to 425°F.

2 Break the RITZ crackers coarsely into a pastry-lined pie pan.

3 Combine the water, sugar, and cream of tartar in a saucepan; boil gently for 15 minutes.

4 Add the lemon juice and the lemon rind to the water-sugar mixture. Cool.

5 Pour the syrup evenly over the crackers.

6 Dot the crackers generously with butter and sprinkle with cinnamon.

7 Cover with the top crust. Trim and flute the edges by pressing all around with a fork. Cut slits with a sharp knife on the top crust to let the steam escape.

8 Bake 30 to 35 minutes until the crust is crisp and golden.

Serve warm.

Why You're Fooled

The distinctive tastes of different foods are due to a number of qualities. These include flavor, temperature, and textures. Vegetarian cooks often try to create meatlike dishes without using meat. I tried the meat recipes and found them close but not exactly like the real thing. One friend who hates chopped liver didn't like the substitute either.

Your tasters will have a hard time figuring out what these dishes are really made from, especially the cracker pie.

Bizarre Shapes and Sizes

LIGHT REFLECTED FROM THE OBJECTS you look at forms an image on a light-sensitive area on the back of your eyeball called the *retina*. The size of an image on your retina depends in part on the distance the object is from your eye. When a man walks away from you, his image on your retina gets smaller. That is a fact. It is also a fact that within limits you are not aware of this change in size. A six-foot-tall man still appears to be six feet tall despite his shrinking image. You interpret the change in the size of the image as a change in distance. Your view of such a shrinking image as moving away from you while remaining the same size is called *size constancy*. Artists use size constancy to create an illusion of depth in a flat picture. The skillful use of the angles of lines and the sizes of objects in a painting gives it depth or "distance perspective." Nearby objects are made larger than those supposed to be distant. A skillful artist can make a flat surface appear three-dimensional. In these pictures the distant figure looks "normal." When it is moved to the foreground it seems surprisingly small.

Suggestions of depth in simple line figures are the bases of many of the classic optical illusions in this chapter. Other illusions included here are caused by the way we judge length. Vertical figures look longer than horizontal ones although they may be exactly the same. Still another kind of illusion is based on the brain and the eyes getting conflicting information. When you look at some of these apparently simple figures, their forms change back and forth as if your brain can't quite make up its mind about what you are seeing. This last sentence is a good example of one that gives no information about why we see what we see. ". . . A brain that can't make up its mind . . ." *profoundly* reveals how little we know about what's really happening.

Enjoy your confusion as you view the illusion.

Simple Challenges to the Eye

A few lines in a figure are hard to interpret.

How to Fool Yourself

Many of the following figures were named for the scientists who discovered them. Look at them and answer the questions.

Which line of the Müller-Lyer figure is longer?

Measure them. The two vertical lines are the same length.

Why You're Fooled

Psychologists state that the information for the length of a line is not simply its length. The angles of the lines at the ends somehow affect our judgment.

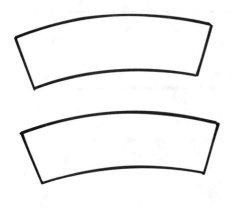

Which shape in this Wundt illusion is larger?

Why You're Fooled

The two shapes are the same size. The upper figure appears smaller because its shorter arc is next to the longer arc of the lower figure. The position makes the upper figure seem smaller.

The sets of long lines in the next two figures are parallel. They appear to bulge in the top illusion (Hering), and cave in, in the bottom one (Wundt).

Why You're Fooled

You can see that the lines are parallel by holding the edge of the page up to one eye so that you are looking down the lines. Close the other eye. The superimposed lines will be too indistinct to be the distraction necessary for the illusion.

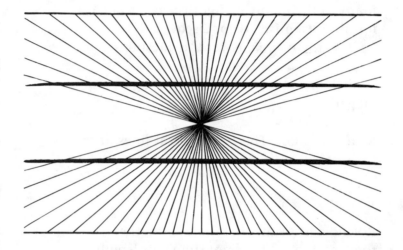

Artists create the illusion of depth in pictures. They draw what appear to be parallel lines, like railroad tracks, but they are at an angle so they meet at some point. This point appears to be in the distance. It is called the *vanishing point* and it creates a horizon.

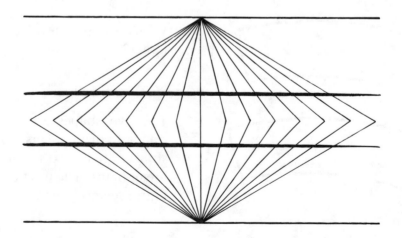

Overrated Height

You may think that this top hat is taller than the width of the brim. If so, you're wrong.

How to Fool Yourself

Look at this picture. Does the hat appear taller than the brim?

Why You're Fooled

One of our common failings is that we perceive height as greater than width even when they are the same. This is called the *vertical-horizontal illusion*. A tree that is standing is estimated as being taller than when it is lying on the ground. Experiment with this when you shop for a Christmas tree.

Here's another way to show you how far off your sense of vertical distance is from your sense of horizontal. Make a dot with a black pen on a sheet of white paper. Make a second dot about one inch directly above it. Now make a third dot along an imaginary line at right angles to an imaginary line between the first two dots so that it, too, appears to be one inch from the original dot. Measure your efforts. How good is your eye at estimating equal distances horizontally and vertically?

One explanation for this misperception is that it takes more effort to raise our eyes up and down to judge height than from side to side to judge width. As a result, we tend to judge height as greater because of the greater effort involved in viewing it.

Alternating Forms

What you see in a figure changes as you look at it.

Study this figure for a while. Do you see a white vase or two black profiles?

Is this "book" opening toward you or away from you?

This figure is called the *Necker cube* after the man who first drew it. Which corner is nearest to you?

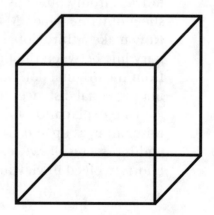

These are three examples of what are called reversible ambiguous figures. All the distance, direction, and contrast cues are equal. As a result, your brain cannot decide what it is looking at, so you see alternate forms that switch back and forth. Sometimes you see the vase, sometimes the profiles; sometimes the book opens toward you, sometimes away from you; sometimes one corner seems close, and sometimes another. You can have some conscious control as to which form you see, but after a while the figure will spontaneously switch back or "reverse" to the alternate form.

One question a scientist might ask is, "What is the rate of switching?" You can time when an image reverses for a subject. The next question might be, "Do these images reverse at the same rate for all people?" It has been suggested that the rate of reversal for these images is faster for highly creative people than it is for less creative people. If you can think up a way to study this question, you have an interesting science fair project.

It is part of our Western culture to be uncomfortable with ambiguity and to regard a figure as more important than the background. Many of us find that looking at these figures is not a pleasant experience. Oriental cultures differ in their perception of such figures. Eastern cultures accept uncertainty and ambiguity. The yin/yang symbol expresses the idea that the figure and the background are meaningless without each other. It would be interesting to see if someone brought up in China or Japan has the same discomfort in viewing these ambiguous figures that Europeans and Americans have.

Impossible Pictures

*See pictures that look real enough but are impossible
to build in the real world.*

How to Fool Yourself

Which is the bottom step of the upper staircase?

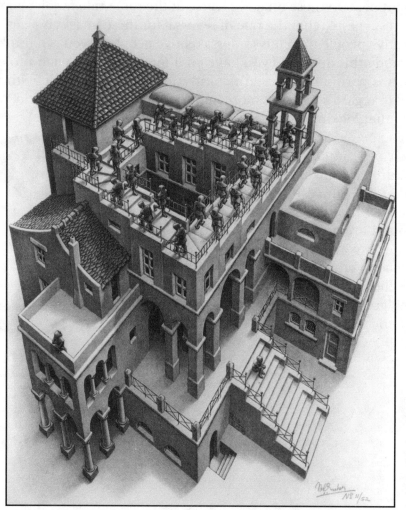

*Ascending and
Descending*
by M. C. Escher.
©1998 Cordon Art,
Baarn, Holland.
All rights reserved.

This drawing is called a blivit.
Where is the middle prong attached?

Which angle of this triangle is closest to you?

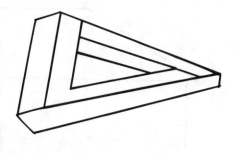

Why You're Fooled

A paradox is the result of two sets of information from the same source that cannot exist together.

When you look at separate parts of each of these figures, they appear possible. You run into trouble when you try to figure out how the whole thing is put together. An artist can put together the clues for depth in a drawing to create a figure that cannot possibly exist in three dimensions. Artist Maurits Escher's (1898–1972) works are famous for their visual paradoxes. When we look at these pictures, we find it disturbing that we cannot construct a mental picture of the "real" object.

A Penny for Your Thoughts

You think a penny will fit where it can't.

How to Fool Yourself

Try to fit a penny on this drawing of a table so that it doesn't touch any of the lines.

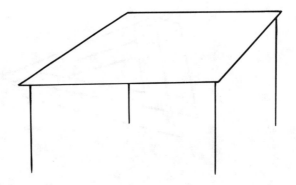

Why You're Fooled

The angles of the tabletop give it an illusion of depth that makes it seem larger than it really is.

The actual geometric shape is smaller than the penny. Would you be fooled if there were no legs on the table? Or does it make no difference?

The Moon Illusion

See the moon appear to shrink as the night wears on.

How to Fool Yourself

Observe a full moon when it first rises, then look at it again later on in the night.

Why You're Fooled

A full moon looks much larger when it is just rising than later on in the night when it is high in the sky. Its *apparent* size has been measured as 1.2 to 1.5 times larger on the horizon than at its zenith. This is one of the classic illusions of all time. If you photograph the moon on the horizon and

then high in the sky from the same location and measure the diameters, they will be the same. In fact, the photo of the moon at the horizon will be a disappointment. It will not have the large, looming presence it has in real life.

The enlarged size of the moon is related to seeing the moon close to familiar distance cues in front of the horizon. These cues are not available when it is high in the sky. When the moon is near the horizon, look at it through a tiny window made by pressing together the thumbs and forefingers of both hands held up to the eye. The window blocks out everything but the moon, which immediately shrinks in size.

Straightening Out Your Mind's Eye

See an interrupted line appear not to line up.

Is one slanted line in this figure a continuation of the other? If they look as if they are not continuous, you are seeing the Poggendorff illusion. Poggendorff discovered that when a slanted line is interrupted by two parallel lines, its separated halves look as if they wouldn't meet each other.

Why You're Fooled

There is a complicated explanation for this illusion that has to do with the way we estimate angles. If the crossing line is at right angles to the parallel lines, we have no trouble seeing that they meet. As the angle changes from 90° we have increasing problems seeing that they meet.

You can, however, straighten yourself out. While looking at the illusion, imagine a hand pulling at each end of the slanted lines as if they were having a tug-of-war with a rope. As the tension increases, watch as the rope straightens out across the gap.

The Ames Window

A window you know to be rotating appears to be waving back and forth. A pencil stuck through one of the openings seems to bend around the window.

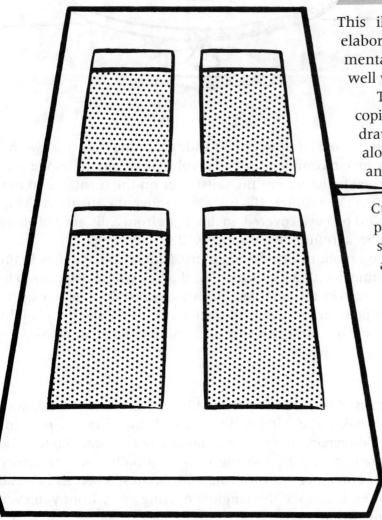

This illusion involves a fairly elaborate setup and some experimentation, but the results are well worth it.

Trace or make two photocopies of the trapezoid window drawn here. Cut them out along the heavy dark outline and trace the shape on a piece of cardboard. Cut out the cardboard and paste a trapezoid on each side. Cut out the shaded areas to make openings in the window. Mount the window by sticking a long toothpick between the paper and the cardboard and the balance point indicated in the diagram. The toothpick will hold its position if you use enough paste. Make a stand for the "window" by sticking the end of the toothpick into a saltshaker.

The illusion is created by slowly and steadily rotating the window on a turntable. One source recommended two revolutions per minute. We used a lazy Susan turned by hand. Put the saltshaker on the turntable so that the toothpick is over the center. Have a friend move the turntable while you observe it, with one eye covered, in dim light from a distance of about ten feet. A plain background, like a white wall surface, helps.

Here are some variations that are fun to try: Observe the window in the dark by illuminating it with a flashlight. The shadow will also appear to be waving back and forth instead of rotating. Stick a pencil through one opening and tape it in place or put a red dot on one side of the small end of the trapezoid. The effect is so dramatic that it's hard to describe in words.

Why You're Fooled

This illusion is caused by a conflict created by the shape of the window. The narrow end makes the window look as if it is a rectangle pointing away from you. Converging lines are a distance cue for parallel lines. You saw this in the railroad tracks and the vanishing point used by artists. When the smaller end moves toward you, your brain still perceives it as if it were at the far end. You see the window moving away from you even when it is moving toward you.

Brightness Mad and Color Crazed

EVER NOTICE HOW DIFFICULT IT IS to see when you enter a dark theater on a bright day? For the first few minutes you can't see much of anything. This is the first period of what scientists call "dark adaptation," a process that has two distinct stages. The first stage is the rapid change that is completed after about seven minutes. At the end of this period you can see your way around the theater, but your vision is not very sharp. The second stage of dark adaptation begins after twelve minutes, and you'll notice that you are able to see an increasing amount of detail. After forty-five minutes, you'll be seeing about as well as you possibly can in dim light, although some scientists claim that slow improvement continues for up to twenty-four hours.

Your adjustment to bright light, after being dark-adapted, on the other hand, is very rapid. Your eyes may hurt, and you'll be temporarily blinded when you reenter the street after you've been in the theater. But the adjustment is complete within two minutes.

The double-adaptation process is due to two kinds of receptors in the eye. The center of the retina contains receptors called *cone cells,* which are sensitive to bright light and to colors. Night vision is the work of receptors called *rod cells,* which are found surrounding the central area. There is some overlap between the sensitivity of rods and cones that makes you susceptible to illusions at low illuminations. Also, the contrast between bright areas and dark areas is often a source of confusion. Bright areas are seen as larger than dark. Light-colored shapes seem larger than dark-colored shapes. The French discovered this illusion when they designed their three-colored flag. Originally the flag had three vertical stripes of equal width: one blue, one white, and one red. But the blue stripe looked wider than the red one, especially when the flag was full-sized, not small on paper. So the flag was redesigned in the proportions of 30, 33, and 37. Now the stripes look equal (see the cover of this book).

Colors also appear different, depending on what is next to them (no secret to artists!). Look at the illustration on the cover where the purple band is in the middle between a red band and a blue band. The purple band doesn't appear to be uniform in color. It looks bluish next to the red band and reddish near the blue one. Cover the red and blue bands, and you'll see that the purple band is, indeed, uniform. Artists use the effect of one color on another to create illusions of size and distance.

The illusions in this chapter are based on the strange things that happen in what you might call the twilight zone.

The Case of the Bulging Borders

Brighter is bigger.

Which circle looks larger, the white or the black?

Would you believe they're the same size? (Of course you would, given your experience in reading this book!) In general, bright objects look larger than dark objects. Here's an example from nature. A crescent moon is the brightly illuminated rim of a sphere. Most of the illuminated surface faces away from us. If you look carefully, however, you can see the rest of the sphere because of the reflected light from the earth, or earthshine, on the moon. The arms of the crescent moon seem swollen larger than the dark part of the sphere, giving rise to an old saying that there is "a new moon with the old moon in its arms."

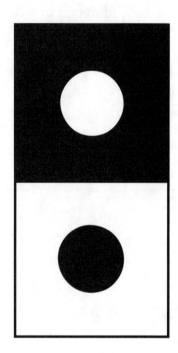

Here are some other examples: The filament of a lightbulb appears to swell when it glows. If you hold a pencil in front of a candle flame, the pencil appears narrower in front of the flame due to the apparent bulging of the background.

Here's one possible explanation that is by no means certain. When bright light falls on the retina, it not only stimulates the cells it falls on but adjacent cells as well. Since there isn't any clear boundary to the image, a spreading effect is the result.

Advertisers design packages in light colors to make them appear larger, and fashion designers suggest that people who are overweight wear dark colors to appear slimmer.

The Hermann Grid

See phantom shadows where none exist.

How to Fool Yourself

Look at one of the black squares. Do you see dark spots where the white bars cross?

Now look directly at an intersection between white bars. The ghostly dark spot disappears when you look directly at it, but the "ghosts" in your peripheral vision remain strong.

Why You're Fooled

This illusion depends on two aspects of vision. The first is that

white appears to be whiter when it is next to black. The white bars between the black squares appear whiter than at the intersections. An intersection is seen as white meeting white and thus appears less white than next to black. Ghostly, darker areas are the result.

The second aspect of vision is that the cone receptors respond more accurately to bright light than do rod receptors. Cone cells are located in the center of the retina. When you look directly at the intersection, you clearly see that no dark area exists. The rods in the peripheral field of vision are responsible for the illusion. They demonstrate a phenomenon called *inhibition*. Receptors that are firing inhibit neighboring receptors from firing, thus producing areas of darkness.

This theory, by the way, is in conflict with the theory explaining the last illusion. How can receptors stimulate neighboring receptors in one case and inhibit them in another? The answer is that there are multiple layers of interaction with neighboring nerves going on at the same time. Some of them cause enhanced stimulation, and some of them inhibit stimulation. Clearly, understanding how we see is quite complicated.

The Cornsweet Illusion

See how a white disk is brighter in the center, but only when it is whirling.

How to Fool Yourself

You will need a flat, white paper plate about 6 inches in diameter (I cut out the center of a 10-inch paper plate), scissors, tape, and some kind of rotating motor such as a hand mixer or electric drill. Cut out a wedge with a spur next to a notch in the plate as shown in the illustration for disk 1. Make a central hole slightly smaller than the diameter of the shaft of the mixer beater or drill bit. Cut two small slits in the hole as shown. This will make the disk fit snugly around the shaft of the beater or drill bit.

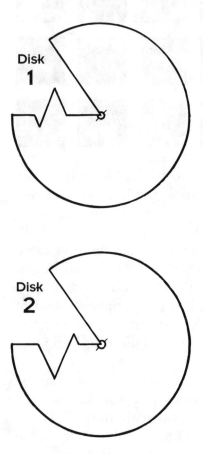

NOTE: There is some danger of getting hurt if an electric drill or hand mixer is not used properly. Ask for adult supervision before you do this experiment.

Put the disk on the shaft of the beater or drill bit and insert into the motor. Use tape over the slits to keep it in place. Rotate the motor at different speeds. Although the center of the disk and the outer border are illuminated exactly the same amount, the division caused by the spur in the cutout (disk 1) will make the center seem brighter. If you make a second disk as shown, with the spur and notch positions reversed, the border will seem brighter.

Why You're Fooled

The spur of the disk creates a variation that makes the area next to it increase in brightness. The notch creates a local variation that makes the area next to it seem dimmer. If you rotate a disk with a cutout wedge without a spur and notch, or if you cover the spur and notch with a piece of paper taped over the contours, the inside and the outside appear equally bright.

Meyer's Experiment

See a color where there is really only gray.

How to Fool Yourself

Place a small square of gray cardboard or paper on a bright red or green background. Cover both the square and the background with two or three sheets of waxed paper or a single sheet of tissue paper. Gaze at the gray square. If the background is red, the square takes on the complementary color of blue-green. If the paper is green, the square appears reddish.

Why You're Fooled

The illusion of color disappears if the gray square is enclosed in a black outline, or if it is placed on top of the waxed paper. The color within a clearly outlined area is determined by the contrast at its borders. The wax paper reduces the sharp boundary at the border. The gray area, which is colorless, takes on the complementary color of the background—reddish if the background is green or greenish if the background is red. Artists know that colored areas are influenced by the colors next to them.

Benham's Top and Other Spin-Offs

See colors in a spinning black-and-white object.

Copy the black-and-white pattern illustrated here on a white, 4-inch disk. Make the black very black with India ink. Rotate the disk on different devices—from a pencil (if you haven't got anything motorized) to an electric hand mixer. (I stuck my disk to the beater of an electric hand mixer by inserting the beater shaft through the center of the disk and taping the underside of the disk to the beater.)

When you spin the disk (in a strong light) in a clockwise direction, you will see a series of rings ranging from a bluish color on the outside to greenish in the middle and reddish in the center. Reverse the rotation and the color sequence is also reversed. Try this at various speeds. Different people react differently and see colors at different speeds, so be patient until you see the illusion. If you rotate the disk very fast, the entire thing becomes yellowish.

Try rotating the second pattern, which is a variation of the first. The third pattern creates a different effect.

Why You're Fooled

The theory behind the first illusion is uncertain. Some scientists feel that the disk causes white light to hit the retina in interrupted flashes, thus stimulating us to "see" colors. Somehow the flashing lights stimulate the retinal receptors to fire.

The illusion experienced with the third disk is known as Plateau's spiral. When it is spinning fairly slowly, you seem to be either looking into a tunnel or a tunnel is pushing out at you, depending on the direction of the rotation. At high speeds you don't see the tunneling illusion, but the entire disk takes on a rosy glow.

The Purkinje Shift

See colors become extra bright as the light fades.

How to Fool Yourself

Ever notice how grass and trees seem extra bright as the sun goes down or during a summer shower? Yellow tulips appear to be darker and red roses can seem almost black. No, nature has not changed these colors on you. All that has changed is the amount of light on the subjects—twilight has fallen. This phenomenon is known as the Purkinje shift.

You can also see the Purkinje shift if you study a color photograph of a landscape in sunlight and then observe it in dim light. The greens in the picture seem to jump out at you. Jan Purkinje (1787–1869), a Bohemian physiologist, discovered this effect in the early nineteenth century. He noticed the change in brightness while looking at an oriental carpet at dusk.

Why You're Fooled

The Purkinje shift is related to the way our eyes function as they slowly adjust from color vision, which operates in bright illumination, to night vision, which operates in dim illumination. Normally, reds and yellows seem brighter to you in daylight and seem less bright than greens and blues at dusk. For this reason, greens seem unnaturally bright as the light fades.

Phantom Moves

THE HUMAN RACE could not have survived without being able to perceive motion. We had to be able to detect moving objects in order to hunt and to protect us from being hunted. We see movement of both prey and enemy as the real movement it is. Perhaps one of the best demonstrations of the accuracy of human movement perception is in sports. Many ball games require split-second responses to moving balls and opponents. Clearly, such motion is part of reality.

But there is a lot of movement we see as motion that is not movement at all. It's called *apparent motion*. We can also see moving objects as if they were standing still. We misjudge objects we think are moving when these objects are actually motionless. Sometimes we are not sure in what direction an object is moving and the speed at which it is moving. We are perhaps more vulnerable to illusions of motion than illusions of contrast, distance, and color.

Some real motion is invisible to us. We cannot see objects moving as fast as a speeding bullet. Our eyes cannot see the motion of objects that move as slowly as the minute hand of a clock. We know it is moving only because we see its position change over a period of time.

In order for us to perceive motion, at least one of three things must happen, although sometimes all three occur at once. First, if an image moves across our retinas, we perceive motion. Our peripheral visual field is especially sensitive. Often we spot something move—say, an object falling outside a window—out of the "corner of our eye." Second, if we move our eyeballs to keep an image of a moving object in the same place in our visual field, motion is perceived. This activity is called *tracking* and is performed automatically. The final

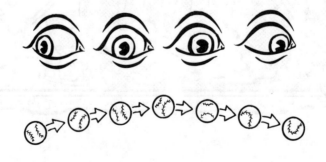

important clue to motion is if we move our head or body to keep an object in sight. There is no doubt in the mind of an observer sitting by the net at a tennis match that the ball is moving. In addition, we all learn how other clues, such as changes in size, brightness, and clarity of an object, indicate motion. For example, we usually interpret a shrinking image as an object that is moving away from us.

The experiments in this chapter will open your eyes to movement that is not real, real motions you cannot see, and a number of other kinds of false moves.

Moves from a Displaced Eyeball

*Produce the illusion of a moving object
with your eyeball.*

Close one eye. Look at an object. Now gently push on the side of your eyeball (on the lid, of course). The object moves around.

Why You're Fooled

You don't for one moment believe that the object is actually moving because you feel your eyeball being pushed into a strained position. But there are many times when the movement of your eyeballs is part of the information by which you perceive motion, although you are not consciously aware that they are moving. For example, whenever your eyes follow a ball flying through the air, you perceive real motion. This is in spite of the fact that the image stays in the same place on your retina.

The motion you perceive with your eyes can be transferred so that you sense your entire body is moving. You may have noticed this in the movies. If the screen shows a road disappearing in front of the hood of a car as if you are viewing it through a windshield, and if you concentrate on the road and ignore visual clues that you are in a theater, you will feel as if you are moving in the car. Some people have difficulty watching motion in very large-screen theaters because they get motion sickness.

Ocular Parallax

See a nearby object jump from one place to another
without really moving.

How to Fool Yourself

Look at something that is about a foot and a half in front of your eyes and alternate opening and closing each eye. If you alternate your eye winks fast enough, the object will appear to dance back and forth in front of you.

Why You're Fooled

The reason for this apparent motion is that your eyes view the object from slightly different positions. The angle of sight makes the object shift slightly compared with its background. With both your eyes open, this difference in position is fused into one image and you see depth. (More on this in the next chapter.) When you look with one eye and then the other, you become aware of the change in position.

In this illusion you know that the object isn't really moving because you are aware of the work your eyes are doing. Parallax is the apparent change in position of an object in the foreground against its background caused by the change in the position of the observer. The slight change in the position of relatively nearby stars against the pattern of background stars was proof that the earth moves. The shift is due, of course, to the changing position of the viewer on earth as the earth orbits the sun. Parallax is discussed again in chapter 8.

Traveling Moon

See the moon travel with you.

How to Fool Yourself

Look at the moon through your car window. It is moving so quickly that it's keeping up with you.

Why You're Fooled

Of course, the moon is *not* moving with you. What you see is an illusion. Nearby objects fly past your moving vehicle. Their position in your line of sight changes rapidly. The moon is so far away that it hardly changes its position relative to your eyes. For this reason, it appears to be moving with you.

The real motion of the moon across the sky, due to the rotation of the earth, is so slow that you don't see it moving. All you observe is its position changing over a period of time.

False Moves

You feel as if you are moving, but you're not.

How to Fool Yourself

You are sitting in a train or plane looking out the window. You see the motion from the train on the next track or from an airport service vehicle, and you feel as if you are starting your journey or pushing back from the gate. Surprise! You are not actually moving. Prove it by looking at the platform or a distant airport building.

Why You're Fooled

This illusion is created by viewing a large moving object that fills your visual field. The train or plane window limits your visual field to a moving object viewed through the window. Your eyes track the moving object as if you were actually moving yourself, thus creating the sensation of whole-body motion.

A similar illusion, called the Duncker effect, is created when you observe an enclosed object through a moving framework or environment. An example is viewing the moon through clouds, where the moon is the enclosed object framed by the clouds. The moon appears to be moving through the clouds, although it is the clouds that are actually moving. The tops of tall buildings may also appear to be moving when seen against a background of moving clouds.

The Waterfall Illusion

*See the banks on the side of a waterfall
rise as the water falls.*

How to Fool Yourself

Gaze at a waterfall for about two minutes. Shift your view to the banks on one side and they will appear to be moving upward. If you watch snowflakes falling, tracking them individually as they move down, and then shift your gaze to the ground, the snow on the ground will appear to rise. The disk with the spiral (see page 63 in chapter 5) seems to shrink when you watch it rotating. When you stop its motion, it will seem to expand in the opposite direction.

Why You're Fooled

This is a kind of afterimage effect. The receptors that perceive motion in one direction get tired. When you stop looking, receptors for motion in the opposite direction are not inhibited from firing. So you perceive motion in the opposite direction.

The first person to scientifically observe this illusion was the famous German physicist Hermann von Helmholtz (1821–1894). In 1860 he noticed something very peculiar after he had been looking out of the window of a moving train for some time. When he shifted his gaze to the inside of the railroad car, it also appeared to be moving, but in a direction opposite to the view of the landscape.

Dancing Star Point

A nonmoving point of light will not stay still when you look at it.

How to Fool Yourself

Lie on the grass on a starry night and try to stare at a single star. It will dance before your eyes, gliding and wandering about in an unpredictable manner.

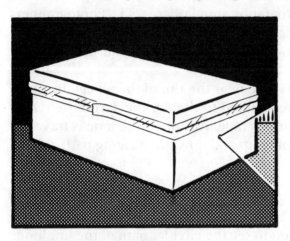

You can see this effect even more dramatically with a simple lab setup. Make a pinhole in a shoe box. Put a lit flashlight in the box and tape the cover down so that it is light-tight. Observe the tiny source of light in a perfectly dark room. It is very important that the room be completely dark and that you have given yourself time to adapt to the dark before observing the light source. The point of light will move in very dramatic ways.

Why You're Fooled

This phenomenon is called the *autokinetic effect,* meaning "self-motion," because one theory states it is caused by the fact that your eyes are never at rest and are continually moving. Most of the time, you are not aware of this motion.

In early aviation history, pilots would keep in squadron formation by staring at the wing light of another plane. Fixating vision at night could lead a pilot to experience the autokinetic effect. He would see a wing light make rapid moves that seemed to show a large change in flight path. The pilot would make quick moves to follow this false path and risked the chance of collisions and spins which could cause a crash.

Planes now use bright flashing signal lights, and pilots are trained to keep their eyes moving and not staring while night flying, in order to reduce the hazards of the autokinetic effect.

Unbending a Circular Path

A spot of light you know to be moving around the rim of a wheel appears to be moving up and down a hill.

How to Fool Yourself

To create this illusion you'll need luminous tape, the kind that glows in the dark. You can buy it where photography supplies are sold. (Photographers use it to mark light switches, etc., in darkrooms.) Some hardware stores also sell it. You'll also need some kind of wheel. You can use a bicycle wheel or the wheel on a toy.

Put a small piece of luminous tape near the rim of the wheel. In a perfectly dark room, after you have adapted to the darkness, roll the wheel across the floor. Watch the luminous tape. Although the tape is traveling in a circle, it will appear to be going up and down in a zigzag path.

Why You're Fooled

There are not enough cues for you to see the circular path of the luminous patch. If you want to get rid of the illusion, simply put another square of tape at the center of the wheel. When your eyes are looking at two reference points, rather than just one, the outside light appears to be traveling around the wheel.

Orbiting Circles

See a drawing of one circle move around another circle that it overlaps.

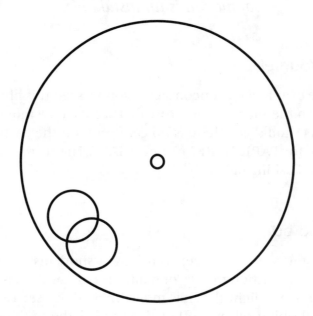

How to Fool Yourself

Cut a 5-inch disk from the center of a 10-inch white paper plate. Draw two overlapping circles, each one inch in diameter, with black ink as shown. Place the disk on a turntable or make a hole in the center and spin it on a pencil. Stare at one of the circles as it rotates. The other circle will appear to be moving.

Why You're Fooled

You will not get this effect if you use squares instead of circles. This illusion is partly due to the fact that a circle has no direction. (Squares have corners.) As a result, there are no clues to its rotation. When you stare at one circle, it seems fixed in place. The other circle appears to be gliding around it instead of really changing positions.

The Phi Phenomenon

*Nothing moves, yet the appearance
of motion is unmistakable.*

How to Fool Yourself

If you've ever looked at neon signs, you've seen this illusion. One example is a sign in the shape of an arrow that seems to be moving in the direction observers should go. There is no confusion on the part of the customer as to where to "PARK HERE" or find "GAS." The secret to this illusion is the timing of flashing lights.

Why You're Fooled

If two light sources are separated by a short distance, and one light is flashed on a fraction of a second after the other flashes off, you see it as a single source of light that has moved. You don't see two separate sources of light flashing on and off. This is called the *phi phenomenon*, and the appearance of movement depends on the length of time between stimuli. If the time between flashing lights is too long, you see them as separate. Movement is perceived, across an empty space, when the interval is shortened. If it is too short, both lights appear to be flashing simultaneously.

Other senses are also susceptible to the phi phenomenon. If a light touch is applied to two nearby points on your skin in rapid sequence, you will feel as if something has moved from one place to the other. If there is a very short time interval (a fraction of a second) between a click close to one ear followed by a click close to the other, you will sense that the sound has moved through your head, literally in one ear and out the other.

Animation and the Movies

See still pictures move.

How to Fool Yourself

Hold the upper right pages of this book together about 1 inch from the corner while you flip the corners of the pages. The book winks at you. This illusion is based on timing. You must see the sequence very rapidly in order to experience motion. Turning the pages as you read this book doesn't work.

Why You're Fooled

Each eye image is like a flash of light. Psychologists have studied the phenomenon underlying motion pictures and animation by finding out just how fast lights must flash on and off before fusing into a steady beam. The number of flashes per second needed to see flashes as a steady light is called the *critical fusion frequency*. The critical fusion frequency varies depending on a number of factors, including the brightness of the light and the amount of time of light versus dark. When the time of the light flash equals the dark period, dim lights fuse at about 15 flashes per second, while bright lights fuse at 60 flashes per second. Fluorescent lights seem like steady light to our eyes, although they are blinking on and off 60 times per second. If a bright light flashes on and off too slowly, you see flickering.

Motion pictures flash 24 pictures or frames per second. We don't see flickering because there is very little dark between frames. That is, there is a much longer light period compared to dark. If the dark between frames on the film were the same size as a frame, you would see flickering. And, if the light is too bright or the film is moving too slowly, the movie will flicker. (Early movies did flicker, and so were called "flicks.")

Animation works on the same principle as motion pictures except that a series of drawings replaces the frames or photographs. Flip books that work by flipping pages are a simple animation device. An early but more sophisticated animator was the zoetrope, a cylinder with slits in it at even intervals. There is a slightly different picture under each slit. When the zoetrope spins, you look through the slits, which are traveling past your eyes fast enough to give you a view of images in a series of rapid flashes. Thus the figure moves.

Stroboscopic Vision

You can read through a dense pattern,
but only when it moves.

How to Fool Yourself

This is an old parlor trick. Draw a grid on a piece of tracing paper as follows. First, with a black pen or pencil, draw a series of parallel lines that are about ⅛ inch apart. They should cover an area at least 5 inches square. Then draw a second series of parallel lines at right angles to the first. Next draw a series of diagonal lines over the other sets. Finally, draw a fourth set of lines in a diagonal in the opposite direction to the last set of diagonal lines. Hard to see through, right?

Place the tracing paper grid over a book and try to read through it. No way! Now give the paper rapid jerks back and forth. Suddenly the words appear and you can read with no trouble.

Why You're Fooled

Motion enables you to see through something that you can't see through when motionless. You can "see through" the blades of a fan when they are moving, and the slats of a picket fence if you are traveling past them. This is called a *stroboscopic effect,* whereby an interrupted image is fused when the interruptions are rapid enough. This is similar to the critical fusion frequency discussed in the last experiment.

Stop Action

*Make the blades of a fan appear to stop
without touching the fan.*

You have to make a device called a *stroboscope,* which creates an interrupted view of an image. Here's how to make one.

Cut out a 5-inch disk from the center of a paper plate. Locate the center by folding a similar paper disk in quarters. Lay the folded disk along the flat one so that the arcs match. Mark the center with a pencil. Trace a faint pencil line from the center to the edge to mark one radius. Cut a slit ⅛ inch wide and one inch long along the radium about ½ inch from the edge.

Use a circular piece of tape (sticky side out) to attach the center of the disk to the end of an electric mixer beater. Observe a spinning fan through the slit as you slowly increase the speed of the mixer. (If the mixer doesn't change speeds gradually, begin observing it at its fastest speed.) When the timing is right, the fan will appear to slow down and even stop.

Why You're Fooled

When the slit is rotating as the same speed as the fan, the slit is catching the image of only one blade. All the rest of the motion is blocked by the disk. Since the rotating stroboscope is moving fast enough to be transparent, you see the blade as stationary. When the stroboscope is not at the exact speed of the fan, the fan can be seen as if it were slowing up. Stroboscopes are used to time fast-moving devices such as car engines.

If you look at a fluorescent light through your stroboscope, you can see it flicker on and off. A fluorescent light is flickering on and off 60 times per second. The stroboscope interrupts the flickering just enough so that you can see it.

You can also see stroboscopic patterns on a television screen. The picture is created by a beam of light that scans the screen in a horizontal direction, flashing a series of dark and light spots at extremely high speed. If the screen is viewed through a strobe, you can see horizontal bars on the screen that appear to move up or down.

Rotating spokes of a wheel also create a stroboscopic effect. So do the frames of movies. Since all wagon-wheel spokes look the same, there is no way to keep track of which way they are rotating. The combination of these factors produces the unusual effect in movies of making wagon-wheel spokes turn backward while the wagon moves forward. You can sometimes see this effect in car ads on television. The car moves forward, while the insides of the wheels turn in the opposite direction.

Be Your Own Stroboscope

See horizontal bars appear on your
television screen when you hum.

How to Fool Yourself

First, let me say that I did not experience this illusion. It was reported in two scientific journals, however, so there must be something to it. Perhaps it will work for you. It's so outlandish it's worth a try.

An American scientist who reported this effect stood about 20 feet from his television set. He saw horizontal bars appear on his screen when he hummed a note around a bass A-flat. The bars migrated up and down as he hummed higher and lower.

A British scientist watched a black-and-white sectored disk on a turntable. He could make the sectors of the disk stop or migrate forward and backward by changing the pitch of the note he hummed.

Why You're Fooled

Apparently, humming makes your retinas vibrate so the effect is similar to that of a stroboscope, only the illusion is created by your own vibrations in your eyes. I may not have seen the effect because my voice is not low enough.

A Sum of the Parts

*You think you're seeing the whole picture,
but you're really looking at only a slice.*

How to Fool Yourself

Cut a slit in a large piece of cardboard 2 inches long and ¹⁄₁₆ inch wide. Place the slit over any picture in this book. Move the slit rapidly back and forth over the picture. You'll have a sense that you are seeing the whole thing, although you are really only seeing a sequence of ¹⁄₁₆-inch slices.

Why You're Fooled

Psychologists believe this illusion gives insight into the way our brains process information. The image on the retina is only the slice. But our brain puts the pieces together, and we perceive the complete image.

The No-Holes Bar

A wooden matchstick passes through the steel bar
of a safety pin before your very eyes.

How to Fool Yourself

This is an old parlor trick whereby it seems that wood passes through steel.
It takes a little preparation.

Cut the head off a wooden match. Insert the point of a large safety pin
through the exact center of the matchstick and close the pin. Move the
matchstick over to the center of the pin.

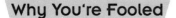

To create the illusion, hold the head of the
pin in your left hand (reverse if you're left-
handed). Rotate the stick so that the top
end is behind the bar of the pin, and
the match is turning on the bottom bar
of the pin. Strike the bottom end of the
match with your right index finger in
a downward motion. The top end of
the match will appear to move
toward you right through the
bar of steel!

Why You're Fooled

Here's what's really happening. By striking downward, you bounce the top
end of the matchstick against the upper bar of the pin. The lower end
moves forward and up. It appears as if the match has moved through the
steel bar because the time interval between the two positions is so short
that you can't see them separately. Also, your experience with the motion
used to strike the match leads you to expect the top part of the stick to
move toward you.

Fast Money

Rub two coins together and see three!

How to Fool Yourself

This is not a get-rich-quick scheme. Like most such plans, this, too, is an illusion.

Get two identical coins. Hold them together between your two index fingers by pressing your fingers together. Rub the coins against each other rapidly up and down. An image of a third coin drops down between the two real ones.

Why You're Fooled

The phantom coin is caused by a slight afterimage left by the real coins, which has not had time to fade. The receptors on your retina will keep sending messages to your brain for a brief period after a stimulus is removed. By continually moving the coins you keep the afterimage going.

Here's a mystery waiting to be solved: no one knows why the image always appears *below* the real coins, not above.

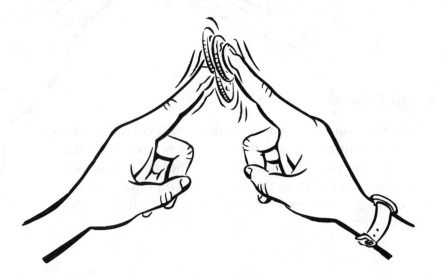

Rubbery Pencil

A wooden pencil suddenly looks like it's made of flexible rubber.

How to Fool Yourself

This illusion depends on your making the right moves. Here's how. Hold the end of the pencil loosely between your thumb and index finger. Shake your hand rapidly up and down so that the pencil wobbles between your fingers. It will seem to become limp and wavy along its length. You can produce the same effect with a butter knife for some after-dinner entertainment.

Why You're Fooled

This is another case where motion produces afterimages on your retinas. The end of the pencil is moving through a wider arc than the middle of the pencil. It is actually moving faster than the middle. The combination of the afterimages at the end of the pencil and the real image in the center produces the illusion of flexibility.

es and
Visual
ities

YOU CAN SEE ALL KINDS OF UNREAL SIGHTS. Perhaps the classic example is a mirage—the illusion of water in the distance that lures the thirsty desert traveler to push on and on in pursuit of a vision that is never reached. Human perception is not completely to blame for such a sight for sore eyes. Mirages are real enough to be photographed. They are caused by the way light is bent as it passes through rising masses of hot air, producing an image of the sky near the ground, an image easily mistaken for water. Thirst may enhance the illusion, but it is certainly not the principal factor. You can see a mirage when you're not thirsty, too. I'll tell you how in this chapter.

There are also visions that are before your eyes all the time that you may not have noticed. These are built into the construction of your eyeball and can be an "insight" into some of the ways your eyes work. Some are sights you can "see" with your eyes closed. Some mean looking deeply into your own eyeballs. You'll find out how to do that, too.

The location of your eyes in the front of your head also gives rise to some peculiar sights. Under the proper conditions you can see holes through solid objects, and you can make two flat pictures combine to form one that has three dimensions, and you can see a three-dimensional picture inside the colorful pattern of a Magic Eye.

And, finally, there are the strange effects of "tired" eyes, after-images of form and color that come from staring at something long enough for your retina to act like film in a camera. When you look elsewhere, the image stays with you for a few minutes before fading.

The eye and nature combine to produce some truly remarkable visual oddities. Be prepared for a sight-seeing tour!

False Ponds

See a mirage on the highway.

How to Fool Yourself

You don't have to be in the Sahara to see this water mirage. All you need is a hot asphalt road and a bright summer day. The best time to look is when you are traveling. Look ahead down the road. When the angle or slope of the road is just right, the roadbed will look wet. It can even act like a mirror and reflect the image of a car passing over it.

Why You're Fooled

The air just above the surface of the road is much hotter than air higher up. Light coming from above is bent when it meets this hotter air, much as light is bent when it passes from air into water. Instead of continuing in its path toward the road, this light is bent up toward your eyes. You see an image of the sky where you would normally see the road. It looks as if the road is covered with a pool of water. What appears to be a reflection of a car as it passes over the mirage is not really a reflection, but the bending of light due to the difference in air temperatures.

Here's another mirage you can look for on a hot summer day. Find a long wall with an even surface. A flat brick wall will do. Put your head against the wall and look down its length. Have a friend stand next to the

wall, about 10 yards from you, holding a bright, shiny object like a key. Watch carefully as your friend brings the key closer and closer to the wall. The image of the key will appear wavy, and the wall itself will act like a mirror reflecting this wavy image of the key. The air next to the wall is warmer than air farther away, thus making the wall act as if it is the shiny, wet surface of water, which can produce mirror images.

Prisoner's Cinema

See the light with your eyes closed.

Gently press a closed eyelid with your fingertip. You will see a glowing circle or semicircle of light directly beneath your finger. Scientists call this sight a *phosphene,* from Greek words meaning "to show light." If you increase the pressure of your finger, you'll see more light in the form of shimmering geometric patterns. An especially good way to generate phosphenes is to close your eyes in the shower and let water strike your eyelids.

Pressure is not the only way phosphenes are produced. In the eighteenth century, people entertained themselves at parties by joining hands, closing eyes, and receiving a shock from one of the newly invented electrical generators. Drugs that produce hallucinations, such as LSD, and alcohol have been known to cause disturbing phosphenes in patients recovering from drug dependencies and alcoholism. Stimulation of the vision center during brain operations causes phosphenes. (Very often patients are conscious during brain surgery. The brain itself has no pain receptors, so local anesthesia is all that is needed to prevent the sensation of pain in the scalp and skull.)

But one of the most interesting examples is the spontaneous occurrence of phosphenes when people have nothing to look at for a period of time. People who lived in dark dungeons reported seeing them—thus giving them the name "prisoner's cinema." Mystics shut off from the world may well be seeing phosphenes when they "see the light" of religious experience. Phosphenes are a hazard to truckers peering into snowstorms for long periods of time. Airplane pilots flying through clouds or at high altitudes during daylight are also susceptible to the annoyance of phosphenes.

Phosphenes are an area of active scientific research. They are caused by the firing of the nerves of vision that usually respond to light stimuli. Their firing when there is no light may be a clue to the orderliness of nerve cells on the retina.

Spots Before Your Eyes

See the spots that are always before your eyes,
although you may not have noticed them.

How to Fool Yourself

The ever-present spots before your eyes are usually invisible because you probably never focused on them under the right conditions. Make a pinhole in a piece of cardboard. Look through it at a bright source of light. You'll see all kinds of transparent circles floating before your eyes.

Why You're Fooled

The spots you observe, which are called *floaters,* are actually old blood cells that are floating in the fluid in your eyeballs. They have broken loose from surrounding tissues and swelled into spheres by absorbing some of the fluid within the eye. The fluid in your eyes is transparent and so are these swollen cells. The pinhole helps you focus on the patterns of light passing through the cell membranes that form the outlines of these floaters.

Ghostly Trees

See a phantom tree on the wall
in a dark room.

How to Fool Yourself

You'll need a flashlight and a dark room. Close one eye and cover it with your hand. Shine the flashlight at the white of the outside of your other eye while you gaze at a blank wall. You might also try blinking the light on and off. After a while, you'll see the image of a leafless "tree" in the dark area of the wall.

Why You're Fooled

This tree is actually an image of the blood vessels on the back of your eye. It is the reflected shadow of the lines blood vessels make on your retina. You can also see it in the morning when you first open your eyes and look at bright sunlight. Before you fully adapt to the bright light, you may catch a glimpse of the shadowy figures of branching blood vessels.

An Eleventh Finger and a One-Eyed Friend

See an eleventh finger, with a fingernail at each end, floating in midair.

How to Fool Yourself

Put the tips of your index fingers together about a foot away from your eyes. Keep your eyes focused on a spot on the wall just above the finger-tips. As you bring your fingers toward your eyes, you'll see a peculiar 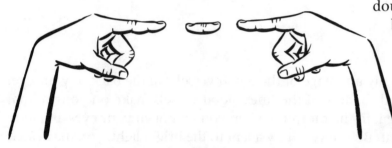 double-nailed finger appear between the tips of your real fingers just below your focused gaze. Draw your fingertips apart, and the eleventh finger will appear to float in midair.

The same kind of focusing can make a friend appear to have one eye. Look straight ahead and focus on a distant spot while you put your forehead and nose against a friend's. Your friend's eyes will appear to be a single eye in the middle of his or her forehead.

Why You're Fooled

When you try to look directly at each illusion, it disappears. Each eye has a slightly different view of the subject you're looking at. You can see this as double vision by holding up your index finger, pointed at the ceiling about a foot in front of your right eye. If you focus on a spot about 3 feet away, you'll see a double image of your finger. Most of the time, when you focus on an object, the two images fuse to produce a three-dimensional view. In these examples, by focusing beyond your fingers and your friend's eyes, the images fuse improperly and create these strange sights.

Magic Eye Viewing

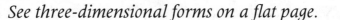

See three-dimensional forms on a flat page.

How to Fool Yourself

It takes some practice to see Magic Eye 3-D images, but the effort is well worth it. The idea is to look past the page into the distance, just as you looked past your fingers in the last trick. Hold a page with a Magic Eye image so that the two dots become three. Let your eyes relax as you do this. Then slowly raise the image so that the pattern is in front of you. If you saw three dots, you will see a 3-D pattern. Another way is to bring the Magic Eye pattern up to your nose. Keep your eyes unfocused and relaxed as you slowly draw the page away from you. The image will appear blurry at first, but as you slowly move it, the pattern hidden as a 3-D image will come into view. Once you can see it, you'll be amazed at how relaxed your eyes are and how easy it is to study it.

Why You're Fooled

Magic Eye creates pictures for 3-D viewing using a powerful computer to merge two patterns in the form of tiny dots with hidden information for each eye. Each eye is getting its own view. The brain combines the information from each eye so that you see depth on the page.

A Hole in Your Hand

*See a bloodless hole through your hand, a book,
a friend's head, or any other solid object.*

How to Fool Yourself

Roll a piece of paper into a tube. Put the tube to one eye and focus both eyes on a distant area at least 15 feet away. Now bring your hand, or some other object, up in front of the eye that is not looking through the tube, still keeping both eyes on the distant object. Move your hand back and forth until you find the exact spot where it appears as if there is a hole in your hand through which you can see the distant object.

Why You're Fooled

This illusion, like the last three, is based on the fact that your eyes are set apart and see slightly different images. When your eyes are focused on a distant object, nearby objects are out of focus, and the image that you see in one eye overlaps improperly with the image you see in the other. You can eliminate this illusion of the hole in your hand by focusing both eyes on your hand. Switch back to the distant object, and again you'll have the illusion that your hand contains a hole.

You can train yourself to ignore the image in one open eye while you concentrate on what you're seeing with the other. Scientists learn to look through the single ocular of a microscope with both eyes open. Keeping one eye shut when you have to study specimens under the microscope for long periods of time causes eyestrain. At first you may be bothered by what you see with the other open eye. But, after a while, you don't even notice those images.

Here's the Limit

Can you tell which of these patterns is made from a single continuous line and which is made up of two discontinuous sections?

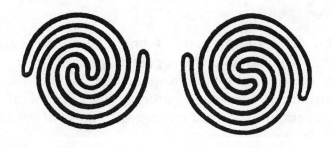

How to Fool Yourself

These patterns are not identical. Can you tell the difference by just looking at them? I don't think so. You must trace the patterns carefully to tell which is which.

Why You're Fooled

These figures were designed by two scientists at the Massachusetts Institute of Technology and are named Minsky-Papert figures, after their designers. They show what the limits of pure perception are, because you cannot tell the difference spontaneously but only with effort.

The limits of pure perception are of interest to scientists because of what they say about human survival. Scientists think that our inability to perceive certain patterns means that such discriminations were not crucial to the survival of early man.

For example, the survival of early humans depended on being able to see a predator against a natural background. If the predator had a natural camouflage that was outside human perceptual limits, early humans could have been in big trouble. An unseen enemy cannot be defended against. Experiments with patterns like the Minsky-Papert figures establish these limits. Then anthropologists and other scientists can apply this information. Perhaps if early humans could not see a particular predator, it was not a threat to them.

Afterimages

Put this bird in the cage by looking at it.

How to Fool Yourself

Stare at the bird for 30 seconds in bright light. Then gaze at the cage. An afterimage of a black bird will appear in the cage.

You can see a color afterimage as well. Look at the dot in the green heart surrounded by a yellow border on the cover of this book. Now stare at a white background. An afterimage will appear of a red heart surrounded by a blue border.

Why You're Fooled

In general, afterimages are caused by continued firings of receptor cells in the eye after being stimulated. There are two kinds of afterimages, positive and negative. These two examples are both negative afterimages. They are produced while the eye is adjusting to the stimulus. The color of an afterimage is explained by a theory that there are receptors which share red-green stimulation and different receptors which share blue-yellow stimulation. When you are looking at green, the red part of the red-green receptor is shut down. If there is a long exposure to the green stimulus, the green part of the receptor keeps firing. When the green stimulus, is removed, the red part of the receptors keep firing (while green recovers), allowing an afterimage to appear. The same process holds for the blue-yellow receptors.

A positive afterimage is caused by a brief exposure to a bright light in an eye previously adjusted to less illumination. You have experienced a positive afterimage when you see a flashbulb light up or gaze briefly into the sun. The positive afterimage quickly changes to a negative one.

Circles from Straight Lines

You can see these straight lines as circles.

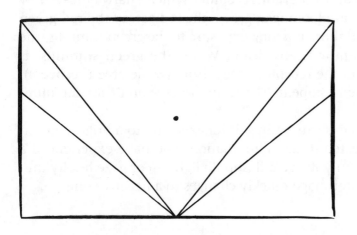

How to Fool Yourself

Copy the four black lines in the diagram onto a 3-inch × 5-inch unlined index card. Spin it at its center on a pen or pencil point. The lines become concentric circles spinning about one another.

You can get an interesting effect if you spin the disk shown below. Make a photocopy of it and cut it out, or trace it onto a white disk. Rotate the disk slowly on a turntable. Notice how the lines become blurred in sections. You can also rotate the disk at high speeds on the end of an electric mixer beater. (I attached mine with a sticky circle of tape at the center of the underside of the disk.) At high speeds all the lines become concentric circles.

Why You're Fooled

Motion plus afterimages produces these illusions. It seems that our eyes tend to focus all the black of the line at some central point. Since each line is a different distance from the center, the concentration of black forms a circular pattern.

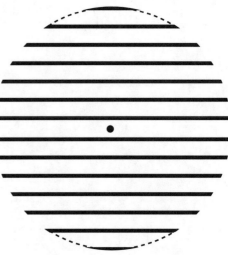

Pepper's Ghost

Make a candle appear to burn in a glass of water.

How to Fool Yourself

This is an old stage trick called Pepper's Ghost. You will need a flat sheet of glass or Plexiglas (I used the removable cover for a record turntable), a glass of water, a lit candle in a holder, and a barrier made by a stack of books.

In a dimly lit area, set up the flat glass or Plexiglas on an angle at one side of the stack of books. Put the glass of water behind it. Now light the candle and place it behind the barrier so that it can't be seen from the front. If you maneuver the candle and glass correctly, the candle will appear to be burning in the glass of water.

Why You're Fooled

This illusion and the ones that follow in this chapter have nothing to do with your perceptions. They are created when light interacts with surfaces and transparent substances. The glass sheet in this stunt does two things. First, it allows light to pass through it so you can see the glass of water behind it. Second, its surface also reflects the image of the candle. When the glass sheet is properly lined up, the reflection of the candle appears to be in the glass of water.

When this trick was used in the theater, an actor offstage cast a reflection on an invisible glass surface. Onstage, it appeared as if the actor were walking through doors and furniture as though he were a ghost.

Distorted Images

See a straight pencil look bent, an image of a coin on the surface of a bowl of water, and the broken shadow of an unbroken pencil.

How to Fool Yourself

Here's how to create the illusions.

1 Hold a pencil partially submerged in a glass of water. If you look at it from the side, it will appear to be bent where it enters the water.

2 Tape a coin securely to the bottom of the inside of a cup or bowl. Slowly back your head away from the bowl until the coin is just out of view. Hold your head in this position as you slowly pour water into the bowl. As the water level rises, the coin will reappear.

3 In a well-lit room, hold a pencil in a basin of water so that it is partially submerged. Look at the shadow cast at the bottom. It will be broken into two segments.

Why You're Fooled

These illusions are all caused by *refraction,* or the bending of light as it passes from one transparent substance—water—to another—air. Light rays are bent as they pass the boundary between water and air toward the surface of the water. As a result, the object they are coming from appears to be in a different place from where it actually is located. If you look down at a person in a swimming pool, his or her feet appear closer than they really are and his or her legs appear shorter.

In the coin illusion, you can't see the coin because some of the light rays coming from the coin are blocked by the cup and the rest of the rays go above your eyes. When you put water in the cup, light that might have been hitting your forehead is bent down toward your eyes and the coin comes into view.

Water clinging to the pencil where it enters the water is bent upward. Light that creates part of the shadow is refracted by this curved surface as if it were a lens. This causes a break in the shadow.

A Flattened Sun

The sun appears flattened as it is about to set.

Observe a sunset carefully where you can see the horizon clearly.

No, the sun isn't really flatter. Its image is bent by our atmosphere in the same way that water bends the image of a stick. The lower the sun on the horizon, the greater the bending of its rays. Light coming from the top of the sun's disk is refracted, so it appears to be higher than it actually is. Your eye assumes it to be where it sees it. A ray coming from the bottom of the sun has to pass through more of the atmosphere because of its lower position, thus it is bent more. So the image of the bottom of the sun is raised more than the top, giving the setting sun a flatter shape.

Great Misconceptions

For centuries people believed that their senses gave a true picture of the earth and its place in the universe. This is entirely understandable given the nature of human perception. Then evidence turned up suggesting that some well-accepted notions were incorrect. Arguments arose defending established views. Some challenges took on powerful institutions, such as the Catholic Church, when they stated different opinions. Sometimes there was violence. In 1600, Giordano Bruno, an Italian philosopher, was burned at the stake for his unconventional views. Traditional ideas die hard even in the face of overwhelming evidence to the contrary.

What destroyed the misconceptions about the earth and the workings of the natural world? A new way of learning called science. Science is a slow process. Bit by bit scientists establish the truth of many facts related to an event or concept. When enough facts have been collected, scientists come to a general conclusion that can change the way we look at a phenomenon. Scientists have been amassing reliable information for the last 350 years, enabling us to know much truth about nature. Scientific instruments, such as the microscope and the telescope, have extended the range and the accuracy of our senses. Scientific experiments have lessened the likelihood of judgments based on prejudice or emotions. Science "sees through" the built-in handicaps of our perception. Interestingly, we use scientific procedures to study ourselves so that we learn to understand our perceptions and their limits better.

Long ago people saw the world in ways that proved to be deeply and profoundly wrong. This chapter tells the stories of some popular illusions that fooled almost everyone. If you had lived in the past, no doubt you, too, would have been fooled.

The Earth Is Flat

Six hundred years ago most people believed that the earth was flat. Why? Because it looked flat. Popular opinion was that the earth was shaped like a round pancake. Land was surrounded by ocean, and a ship would sail off the edge of the earth at the horizon.

Of course, there was evidence that the earth was a sphere if anyone cared to look for it. About 500 B.C. a Greek philosopher named Pythagoras and his followers said that the earth was a sphere. They didn't give any proof, but their views were well thought-out. They obviously had reason to believe that the earth was not flat.

Two hundred years later, Aristotle backed up Pythagoras. During eclipses of the moon, he observed that the shadow of the earth was visible on the surface of the moon. This shadow, Aristotle noted, was always a perfect curve. If the earth were any shape other than a sphere, he concluded, the shadow would not always be such a perfect curve.

There is other evidence in the heavens for careful observers. When a person travels south toward the equator, the North Star (among others) appears to move lower in the sky. At the equator, the North Star is on the horizon, and south of the equator, you can't see it at all. If the earth were flat, the North Star would always be the same height above the horizon, no matter how far south you traveled.

Finally, there is the truth of what really happens to ships when they reach the horizon. You can see for yourself if you are near the sea. Ships seem to disappear, as if they have dropped off the edge of the earth. First, the hull disappears, then the superstructure, finally the masts. And if you take the trouble to watch for ships on the horizon, you will find that they appear from top to bottom in the reverse order. First you'd see the tops of the masts, then the structures on deck, and finally the hull.

All of these observations are indirect evidence for the earth's having a curved surface. But the curve is so large that it can appear flat to human eyes. True proof only came when people sailed around the world. Christopher Columbus set off in 1492 to do this. He believed he could find a new route to India by sailing west. His attempt was halted with the discovery of the Americas. About thirty years later, the task was accomplished by an expedition led by Ferdinand Magellan (ca.1480–1521). One of the ships in Magellan's fleet returned to Spain after a three-year voyage.

Photographs of the earth from space leave no doubt that the earth is a sphere, if anyone is still around to challenge the idea. A person who today insists on believing his or her personal perceptions and refuses to acknowledge the earth is round may well be considered crazy. Six hundred years ago believers in a round earth were in the small minority. They were considered the lunatics.

The Earth Is the Center of the Universe

If you spend some time watching the sky, you will observe that there is motion in the heavens. Every day, the sun rises in the east, moves across the sky, and sets in the west. The moon also rises and sets, as do the stars. The position of the star pattern in the dome of the night sky changes over the year. But when the year is up, the stars are back in the same place they were the year before. The paths of bright bodies called planets also wander across the sky. Their routes are not quite as regular as those of the sun, the moon, and the stars. Occasionally they appear to move backward before moving forward again. But if you spend a long enough time studying the motion of the planets, sooner or later they will return to the spot where you first noticed them. For certain planets, the return to their starting point takes years.

Believing What You See

The first person to study the motions of heavenly bodies in a systematic way was a Greek astronomer named Ptolemy, who was born about a century after Christ. He devised a system of the heavens as he saw it. The earth was motionless, and sun, moon, planets, and stars revolved around it. His system was good enough to predict future positions of the heavenly bodies with as much accuracy as could be viewed with the naked eye, for the telescope had not yet been invented. Ptolemy's system was so successful it became the official position of the most powerful political and spiritual organization in Europe at that time, the Catholic Church.

The earth-centered concept of the universe was the accepted view for well over one thousand years. But even during this time, small inconsistencies not predicted by Ptolemy kept cropping up. Adjustments were made in the system by adding more circles to the paths of the planets. Over time, the Ptolemaic view became more and more complicated.

An Idea Not Directly Observable

In the sixteenth century a new concept of the universe was proposed by Nicolaus Copernicus (1473–1543), a Polish churchman. He had spent over thirty years studying the numbers of the Ptolemaic system. He had also spent some time looking at the night sky. Copernicus's system put a motionless sun in the center with the planets moving around it. The earth was simply another orbiting planet. He explained the motion we observed in the heavens as being caused by two kinds of earthly motion. Not only did the earth move around the sun, but it also rotated on its axis.

In the Copernican system the inconsistencies in the Ptolemaic theory were cleared up. The Copernican plan was so much simpler and everything fell into place. But by stating that it was the earth that moved and by removing it from the center of the solar system, Copernicus challenged common sense and, more dangerously, the official position of the church. His problem was that he had no direct evidence that the earth was, in fact, moving.

Copernicus knew that his idea would cause trouble. He anticipated some of the objections: There was an argument that a moving earth would leave behind birds in flight. Copernicus answered that birds and the atmosphere moved along with the earth. There was an argument that if the earth were moving, we would see the positions of the stars closest to earth change when compared to the pattern made by stars farther away. No such change was observed. (This, by the way, is the idea of parallax I explained in chapter 6 under "Ocular Parallax.")

Copernicus believed that parallax could prove that the earth moved around the sun. If you observe the Big Dipper against a pattern of background stars on March 25, it should look slightly different six months later when the earth has moved halfway around its orbit. Copernicus, of course, couldn't see this *stellar parallax,* and he knew why. He said that the distances between the earth and the stars were so great that there was no noticeable change in star patterns over the course of the earth's orbit. Years after Copernicus's death, measurements through a telescope revealed the expected stellar parallax.

Copernicus feared that the all-powerful church would reject his ideas. He dragged his feet for years before publishing his great book, *On the Revolutions of the Spheres.* In a political move, he dedicated it to the pope. He explained his reluctance to publish in the preface, writing, "I feared I would be laughed off the stage." As it turned out, he didn't have to worry.

He did not see a printed and bound copy of his book until he was on his deathbed.

But, as Copernicus had expected, his book did open a can of worms. The church did reject his system, and his book was put on a list of books that people were forbidden to read. The few people who believed in his system put their careers on the line, even their lives. Giordano Bruno, the Italian philosopher mentioned earlier, was executed in 1600 for supporting the Copernican view of the solar system.

How Truth Triumphed

The support that directly led to the acceptance of the Copernican system came almost one hundred years later. Galileo Galilei (1564–1642), an Italian mathematician and astronomer, refined the telescope and made some amazing discoveries. Among them was the observation that the moons of Jupiter revolved around that planet. This was clear evidence that not everything revolved around the earth, as the church doctrine stated.

Galileo presented his arguments for the Copernican system in a popular and witty book called *The Starry Messenger.* His arguments were so convincing that the church called him a heretic and put his book on its forbidden list. Galileo was brought to trial, publicly condemned, forced to recant his opinion, and sentenced to life imprisonment. But the word was out. And it has stood the tests of time and all the additional information about the universe that has been gathered since Galileo's time.

Objects Come to Rest in
Their Natural Place

Up until the fifteenth century, Aristotle's view of the natural world was the one accepted by educated people. Aristotle based his opinions on his observations, which were subject to error, as he was only human. Of all his misconceptions, perhaps his greatest one was his concept of motion.

According to Aristotle, all matter was made up of four elements: earth, air, fire, and water. All matter possessed one or more of these elements and each element had its natural place. Fire was the highest, air was under fire, water was under air, and earth was at the bottom. All objects would move to their "natural" place depending on the elements they possessed. So, fire rises through air, air rises through water, and earth falls through all three.

There was a lot of common sense to support Aristotle. Water bubbles up through earth. If you add fire to water, steam forms and rises through air. When steam loses some of its fire, it falls back onto the earth as water. In addition to their "natural" motion of moving to their place of rest, objects could also have violent motion as a result of some event. Throwing a stone gives the stone violent motion, but then natural motion takes over until it returns to its natural place. Nice theory, if you don't look too closely.

Galileo Introduces Experiments

In the sixteenth century, Aristotle's views on motion were questioned. In the seventeenth century, they were put to rest by Galileo, whose examination of motion made him "the father of modern physics." Galileo not only challenged the idea that all objects move to their "natural" place of rest, but that rest itself is a natural state. He claimed that an object in motion should remain in motion forever under ideal circumstances. Such an idea of continuing motion on earth is hard to imagine, even today. Moving objects on earth, if left alone, eventually do come to rest.

To back up his idea, Galileo presented a "thought experiment" which is an example of logic at its best. Here is his basic argument:

1 When a ball rolls down a hill, it rolls faster and faster.

2 If you give a ball a shove so that it rolls up a hill, it rolls more and more slowly, until it comes to a brief stop before rolling back down a hill.

Conclusion: A ball rolling on level ground should not pick up speed or lose speed. It should keep rolling at the same speed forever. That it does *not* keep rolling is because of an additional factor.

Galileo correctly figured that friction in the real world prevented balls from rolling forever. He put us on the road to a true understanding of motion, which now states that some external force is the cause of a *change* in either a state of motion or a state of rest. He removed forever the idea that inanimate objects had a "desire" to return to their natural place.

Heavy Objects Fall Faster

Aristotle really went out on a limb when he said, ". . . [if] one weight is twice as heavy as another, it will take half as long to fall . . ." Obviously trusting his senses, there is no evidence that Aristotle ever tested this idea. Galileo did and proved, contrary to what you might think, that all bodies fall at the same speed regardless of weight.

There is a legend that Galileo checked this idea out in a public demonstration, dropping unequal weights off the Leaning Tower of Pisa. There is no evidence that he actually performed this test, although he wrote of such an experiment. He pointed out that the two objects would arrive at the ground at almost the same time. If there were a small difference in impact, it was not as important as the closeness in arrival time.

The First Physics Lab

Galileo had problems in studying falling bodies because in his day there were no timing devices accurate enough for split-second timing. He ingeniously got around this problem by creating a kind of slow-motion device for falling objects. He rolled balls down slanted boards. He reasoned that the change in speed of a rolling ball was similar to its change in speed when falling freely. In other words, the *rate* of change in speed was the same for both cases. Since Galileo was able to measure distance and he could use a dripping-water clock to measure time, he could measure speed (distance divided by time). He found conclusive evidence that all objects fall at the same rate (if there is no resistance from the air) regardless of their weight.

In modern times, an astronaut dropped a feather and a golf ball at the same instant on the moon, where there is no atmosphere to interfere. Sure enough, both reached the ground at the same time.

Index

nerve cells. *See* receptors
night vision, 56, 64
nose. *See* smell

ocean sounds, 26, 27
ocular parallax, 69, 110
optical illusion. *See* vision
orbiting circles, 75

pain, 91
paradox, visual, 49
parallax, 69, 110
parallel lines, 52, 54
past experience, 4, 28
pattern discrimination, 97
pendulum, 17
Pepper's Ghost, 101
perception
  definition of, 4
  limits of pure, 97
  See also specific senses
phi phenomenon, 76
phosphenes, 90–91
planets, motion of, 109
Poggendorff illusion, 52
points, feeling two, 13
positive afterimage, 99
"prisoner's cinema," 91
Ptolemy, 109, 110
Purkinje, Jan, 64
Purkinje shift, 64
Pythagoras, 107

rain sound effect, 27
reality, 2–4, 14
receptors, 3, 8
  for motion, 72
  for smell, 22, 34
  for taste, 22, 33, 36
  for vision, 56, 59, 99
refraction, 103, 104
resonance, 26
retina, 42, 56, 58, 63, 82, 83, 86, 91

rod cells, 56, 59
Rumor (game), 30

saliva, 22
saltiness, 23, 33, 36
science, 106
seashell, surf sounds in, 26
seeing. *See* vision
self-awareness, 14
self-motion, 73
sensation, 2, 3, 16
senses, 2–5, 106
  listing of five, 2, 8
  See also specific senses
shape, 3
shrinking image, 42, 67
signature, 18
size, 3
  constancy, 42
  illusions of, 12, 51, 58
skin, 3, 13, 15, 16
smell, 2, 3
  sensitivity of, 22–23
  taste linked with, 23, 34, 35
softness, 15
solar system, 109–11
sound effects, creating, 27–28
sounds, 2, 3, 22
  illusion experiments, 24–32
  localization of, 25
  phi phenomenon, 76
  selective hearing of, 30
sound waves, 29
sourness, 23, 33
speed, falling rate, 114–15
sphere, earth as, 107–8
spinning, 20
  color effects, 60, 62–63
  lines turned to circles, 100
  shrinking illusion, 72
stellar parallax, 69, 110
stickiness, 15
stimuli, 3, 4